# Contents

**Introductory Note** — 2
*by Fred Feldman*

**Section One: Father Coughlin, Fascist Demagogue** — 5
*by Joseph Hansen*

**Section Two: Mayor Frank Hague of Jersey City, New Jersey**

1. Boss Hague's Police Kidnap Norman Thomas — 18
   May 7, 1938, *Socialist Appeal*

2. Hague's Rule Still Awaits Real Challenge—Free Speech Fight Imperative — 19
   May 14, 1938, *Socialist Appeal*

3. Hague Frustrates Meeting Plan—CIO Must Take Lead in Struggle — 21
   June 4, 1938, *Socialist Appeal*

4. How Hague Rules (abridged) — 23
   *by James Raleigh*
   June 4 and June 11, 1938, *Socialist Appeal*

5. Jersey City: Lesson and Warning — 26
   *by James P. Cannon*
   July 9, 1938, *Socialist Appeal*

6. Leon Trotsky on Hague: Excerpts from a June 7, 1938, Discussion — 29

**Section Three: McCarthyism**

1. McCarthyism: An Editorial — 33
   January 18, 1954, *Militant*

2. Fascism and the Workers' Movement — 36
   *by James P. Cannon*
   March 15–April 26, 1954, *Militant*s

3. Draft Resolution on the Political Situation in America (excerpt) — 45
   SWP *Discussion Bulletin* A-20 in 1954

4. McCarthy—A 'Bourgeois Democrat'? A Reply to Vern and Ryan — 54
   *by Joseph Hansen*
   SWP *Discussion Bulletin* A-25 in 1954

# Introductory Note

The end of the post-World-War-II economic boom marked an historic turning point for U.S. capitalism. The rulers are trying to make working people pay for the economic crisis by reducing living standards, degrading working conditions, and slashing social services.

The SWP political resolution adopted in August 1975, *Prospects for Socialism in America*, states: "This will inevitably lead to a sharpening of the American class struggle in all its forms and to deepening class polarization. While the tempo of this polarization cannot be predicted, its general features are clear. Millions of workers will search for the road to independent political action and will more and more turn to class-struggle methods. On the other hand, rightist demagogues and fascist movements pretending to offer 'radical' solutions to the capitalist crises will come forward as candidates for power." (Quoted from *Prospects for Socialism in America,* by Jack Barnes et al. [New York: Pathfinder Press, 1976]).

The documents and articles in this volume examine the characteristics of three significant incipient fascist trends that appeared in the United States during the depression of the 1930s and the cold war witch-hunt of the 1950s.

Father Coughlin's Social Justice movement, Frank Hague's dictatorial antilabor regime in Jersey City, New Jersey, and Senator Joseph R. McCarthy's anticommunist crusade are described and evaluated.

Coughlin, Hague, and McCarthy never succeeded in building an organized mass movement as did Hitler and Mussolini. Nor did they win ruling class support to the same degree as the German and Italian fascists. Instead, the development of these fascist formations was cut off at an early stage.

Instead of turning to fascism in the 1930s, the ruling class extricated itself from the depression by means of a world war.

In the 1950s, the ruling class turned away from head-on confrontation with the Soviet Union after the Korean war and wartime prosperity was extended into peacetime. As a result, McCarthy lost both his usefulness to the ruling class and his mass support. As the SWP 1975 political resolution states, "McCarthyism, which was an extension of the cold-war antilabor policies and loyalty purges initiated by Truman, had an incipient fascist logic of its own that eventually proved counterproductive to the ruling class. The reactionary Wisconsin demagogue had his wings clipped" (*Prospects*, cited above).

Study of these movements provides lessons for working people about fascism and the fight against it. It demonstrates that American fascism, as it appeared in these instances, was not a carbon copy of the fascist movements led by Mussolini in Italy and Hitler in Germany. On the contrary Coughlin, Hague, and McCarthy sought to build an *American* fascist movement, arising out of the American class struggle and appealing to American prejudices. Thus, their movements had characteristics that were very different from the German Nazis and the Italian fascists, while sharing their antilabor and antidemocratic essence.

A look at the role and nature of these movements helps place the current weight and importance of fascist groups in the United States into proper perspective. While fascist and fascist-like organizations ranging from the Ku Klux Klan and the National Socialist White People's Party to the National Caucus of Labor Committees ("U.S. Labor Party") have made some gains from the current racist offensive, none has achieved a substantial mass base. It remains to be seen whether any of these groups or some new formation will emerge as the leadership of a mass fascist movement in the United States.

Farrell Dobbs states in the Education for Socialists publication, *Counter-mobilization: A Strategy to Fight Racist and Fascist Attacks*, "The capitalists are very happy to use the far-out types we run into today. They cause some confusion, stir things up a little, and plow a little ground for a more serious development of fascism. But they are not the real animal we will be fighting when the combat gets really tough."

The materials in this collection demonstrate the ineffectiveness of the class-collaborationist practices of the trade-union bureaucracy in combatting fascist attacks. In the 1930s, these reformists counted on capitalist politicians like President Franklin Roosevelt and New York Mayor Fiorello La Guardia to protect them from fascism. In the 1950s, they supported the policies of the Democratic witch-hunters against the Republican witch-hunters. They went so far in trying to placate McCarthy as to carry out their own witch-hunts in the unions. Such policies led to setbacks for labor, even though in these cases the fascist movements were stopped far short of taking power.

The SWP on the other hand always fought for a strategy of working-class independence on the political arena and for working-class counter-mobilizations against the fascists. It has advocated the right of self-defense against fascist terrorists.

This publication is the third in a series of Education for Socialists publications on American fascism. Taken together with *Counter-mobilization: A Strategy to Fight Racist and Fascist Attacks*, by Farrell Dobbs and *The Fight Against Fascism in the USA*, this volume is a useful introduction to the problems of analysis, strategy, and tactics involved in the working-class struggle against fascism.

Thanks are due to Brian Shannon for his assistance in selecting the items included in this series.

*Fred Feldman*
JULY 1976

# SECTION ONE

## *Father Coughlin: Fascist Demagogue*

*Father Coughlin: Fascist Demagogue,* by Joseph Hansen was issued in pamphlet form by Pioneer Publishers in 1939. It is based on a series that appeared that year in the *Socialist Appeal.*

Father Charles E. Coughlin's "Social Justice" movement was the most influential of the fascist movements that began to gain adherents when the sharp economic downturn of 1937 and 1938 revealed the bankruptcy of the New Deal. The development of these fascist currents was cut off by the opening of World War II. The economic upturn produced by war preparations and the wave of patriotic sentiment directed against the Nazis combined to ease the political crisis facing the capitalists and to considerably reduce the fascists' audience.

As a gesture toward Roosevelt, Coughlin's superiors in the Catholic hierarchy barred him from participating in politics in 1942 and he eventually sank into obscurity.

# FATHER COUGHLIN: FASCIST DEMAGOGUE
By Joseph Hansen

**The rise of the 'radio priest'**

In the summer of 1926, an obscure Catholic priest began broadcasting over the radio in Detroit.

For three years he spoke steadily without gaining any following beyond a local one. His speeches were not particularly striking. He said nothing to distinguish himself as *different* from hundreds of others who performed for America's loudspeakers.

Then the 1929 crash ushered in the worst depression United States capitalism had yet experienced.

Something *different* did occur then. The obscure priest launched a series of violent attacks against "communism." His name zoomed into the national spotlight.

He began broadening his activities like a business man who has succeeded in selling a huge issue of stock for a newly formed company.

In the lowest depths of the depression, he built himself a million dollar shrine. He began publishing a sleek magazine that carried not a line of advertising, yet sold for only a dime—an editor's day dream come true. He organized a wide political movement. He added radio stations to his network until today forty-eight are broadcasting his speeches—at an estimated cost of $8,000 each—to an audience that may number millions.

Big Business tycoons count him an intimate. Many Congressmen consider him the greatest political force outside the White House. Fascists the world over hail him as among the chief of their dark number.

The labor movement has denounced him repeatedly.

This is the Reverend Charles E. Coughlin.

**Political checkerboard**

The political program he has followed is as astounding as his rise from obscurity.

At first the "radio priest" urged his listeners to put their trust in President Herbert Hoover, the "great engineer." As late as January 11, 1931, he declared that "we have lost no faith whatsoever" in President Hoover and his cabinet.

Then he switched to the New Deal and supported it so eloquently that he became one of the most influential spokesmen for the Roosevelt Administration.

"*Roosevelt or Ruin*" was his slogan.

Millions believed him and chose *Roosevelt.*

On November 11, 1934, shortly after the rise of Adolph Hitler to power in Germany, he launched his organization, the National Union for Social Justice. He wrote the program for this organization himself. It has never elected him as its leader or constituted itself on democratic lines. Political discussion at its unit meetings is strictly forbidden. Coughlin is self-appointed supreme dictator.

In the 1936 presidential campaign he switched from the New Deal and supported William Lemke for president.

When Lemke was beaten at the polls, the "radio priest" retired from public life. But his retirement was only temporary.

He came back on the air with a new twist to his political program—*against the Jews . . . revolution . . . prepare for violence. . . .*

Now his movement is spreading from coast to coast. In every city unemployed youths hawk his magazine *Social Justice.* He is conducting an essay contest with prizes amounting to $16,000.

Many people consider him the only hope, the only way out of the depression. Many others consider him the most dangerous menace yet to appear on the American political scene.

**Father Coughlin promises**

The magazine and the radio speeches, copies of which Father Coughlin mails out free by the hundreds of thousands, are designed to appeal to those who have been crushed by the depression—the millions of unemployed, youth who see only a blank future, farmers facing ruin, those who see no more hope in Roosevelt's New Deal.

"I am for a just annual living wage," he declares. "I am for labor's right to organize. I am for the cost of living being maintained on an even keel; and I am for preferring the sanctity of human rights to the sanctity of property with government's chief concern for the poor."

Who could be against a program like that?

But Father Coughlin was not the first man to stand for labor's right to organize, nor the only one to point out the high cost of living. Father Coughlin is not the first orator to round out pungent and stinging phrases about the sanctity of human rights.

Why should a program so commonplace as that create such excitement and clamor, and out of an obscure priest create a national political figure with apparently unlimited funds at his disposal?

*Because that is not his real program.*

**Coughlin and the New Deal**

At one time, if your memory goes back as far as President Roosevelt's election campaign, the New Deal promised these very same things.

And Father Coughlin backed the New Deal one hundred per cent.

> "The international bankers are on their way out," he promised, side by side with Roosevelt. "The prosperity identified with the year 1926 is not too far distant."
>
> "March 4th, 1933! What a memorable day that was! It was the birthday of the 'new deal.' On that date a voice went ringing around the world announcing a new Declaration of Independence. Before the minds of the millions who listened there was revived the drama of Christ as He lashed the money-changers from the Temple." (*The New Deal In Money*, p. 36.)

Father Coughlin described Roosevelt to his rapt followers as the *"New Lincoln,"* the *"protector of the common people,"* and he declared himself ready to follow *"our leader to the end."*

> "I still proclaim to you that it is either 'Roosevelt or Ruin.' I support him today and will support him tomorrow." (Radio Speech, March 11, 1933.)

Father Coughlin even held a number of secret conferences with "New Lincoln" Roosevelt himself. The nature of those conferences has not been divulged to this day. Frequently he called the President's personal secretary over long-distance telephone.

High, wide, and handsome, Coughlin rode the great wave of popularity that swept Roosevelt into office amidst golden promises.

Roosevelt was going to end the depression, put everybody to work, give everybody an annual wage, permit labor to organize, and MAINTAIN PRIVATE PROPERTY.

Coughlin was a key man in the propaganda machine that deluded the people into supporting Roosevelt.

Father Coughlin, the Detroit spell-binder, was a fellow-traveler of Roosevelt's, a high pressure salesman of his wares. When he abandoned the job it was taken over by Stalin's Communist Party.

Of course, Coughlin has since turned against Roosevelt. His reason was very simple.

Highly sensitive to the moods of the masses, Coughlin understands that Roosevelt's answers no longer satisfy the people, especially the unemployed. They are restlessly seeking a way out. Coughlin is not blind to the finger writing Roosevelt's doom on the wall.

The obscure "radio priest" of 1926 has come a long way. The future seems bright for his particular talents. Strife and dissension, wars and rumors of wars, these ring a sweet clangor in the ears of Father Coughlin.

**Capitalism is bankrupt**

One of the surest signs that a social system is mortally sick is the existence of a large body of permanently unemployed workers. Greek civilization toppled amidst the frenzied despair of her unemployed. The broken pillars of the Coliseum in Rome still stand as a monument to the tyrants of the mighty Roman empire who vainly attempted to trick the hordes of unemployed out of their hunger. During the death agony of feudalism, all Europe was wracked by wandering bands of desperate and starving unemployed.

American capitalism is mortally sick.

For ten years, since 1929, capitalism has cast off an increasing number of people whom it can never employ, whom it *cannot even feed*—despite the fact that the land is bursting with food and crops are rotting on the ground.

Each year an estimated 500,000 youth reach employable age and are thrown into the ever-swelling ranks of the unemployed. These hungry, ill-clothed Americans number now almost 17,000,000—a colossal figure!

At first they listened to the promises of Roosevelt's New Deal and these promises sounded good. He was going to feed them, clothe them, give them jobs and security.

Now they know that he lied. Now they know that he cheated them, that he had nothing to give them but increased misery.

The unemployed stand for the moment, uncertain what road to take next. They are starving in the richest country in the world. Warehouses are crammed to the roof with goods. Billions in gold lie idle in the banks. Factory gates are shut. Machines are silent. Crops are plowed under.

Using the LIE that private industry will provide jobs, Roosevelt's *slash relief* program hurls fresh million after million of Americans into the streets. There they may eat garbage—if they can find any left in the garbage pails—while they hunt for a job in private industry.

All about them they see incalculable wealth monopolized and enjoyed by a miserable handful of parasitic stockholders.

The unemployed go hungry.

They are bewildered, but one basic truth they do understand: *This situation is intolerable.*

They are ready for action. No more postcards to Congress! Already they feel in their minds the thing that is coming . . . *revolution . . . three square meals a day . . . clothing . . . a decent home . . . plenty for all . . .*

Democratic capitalism is doomed. Coughlin knows it. Big Business knows it. Roosevelt knows.

Everybody knows it but that wooden skull minority composed of John L. Lewis, William Green, Earl Browder, an idiot or two, and a handful of old maids of both sexes who were left over from the last century. This minority still believes that democratic capitalism will continue indefinitely to punch its meal ticket!

In America apt students have watched the rise to power of Mussolini and Hitler. They understand that only one road is left open to capitalism that has become sour and rotten with old age. In Italy Mussolini called it fascism. In Germany Hitler called it Nazism. We do not yet know what name a similar movement in America might bear. Perhaps in America it will be called—*Social Justice.*

## What is fascism?

Fascism is a combination of two things.

First, it is a wide mass movement of farmers and small business men who face bankruptcy, of youth denied a future under capitalism, of sections of the unemployed. All these layers of the oppressed who are seeking desperately to put their hands on the surrounding plenty become hypnotized by the silver-plated promises of a demagogue who regiments them into blindly obedient shock troops.

Secondly, it is financed and controlled by the very capitalists who above all are anxious to keep the revolutionary violence of the masses from turning against them. In America—the DuPonts, the Morgans, the Rockefellers—the Sixty Families.

To the rank and file followers of fascism, at first it seems a genuine revolutionary way out of their misery. They discover the truth *too late.*

The capitalists provide the money. The dictator provides the powerful slogans, the stirring names, the demagogic program, the organization, the lieutenants, and the *oratory.*

## Father Coughlin's real program

A few years ago it was very difficult to prove that Father Coughlin was *consciously* plotting to build a fascist movement in the United States. But now he has come out more in the open. He has had time to make slips in his public and private utterances. It is only necessary to read his speeches and his magazine *Social Justice* with a little care to discover

Father Coughlin's REAL program.

Only one month before he launched the National Union for Social Justice he said to Paul Weber of Hearst's International News Service (*Detroit Times*, October 10, 1934): *"I am devoted to capitalism."*

Among his sixteen points for Social Justice he calls for the *preservation of private property*.

Devotion to capitalism and preservation of private property—this is the holy Bible of fascism.

On March 13, 1938, in a broadcast over his network, Coughlin urged the establishment in the United States of a *"corporate state,"* which is the gilded way of describing Mussolini's fascist state.

> "A corporate state in which parties would be abolished and the President would be chosen by a House of Representatives elected by occupational classes was proposed Sunday by Father Charles E. Coughlin." (United Press dispatch in the *New York World Telegram* March 14, 1938.)

But he has been more frank even than this. In a signed article in the February 13, 1939, issue of *Social Justice* (page 7) he declared:

> "I am beginning to understand why I have been dubbed a 'Nazi' or a 'fascist' by the Jewish publications in America; for practically all the sixteen principles of social justice are being put into practice in Italy and Germany."

Like all true fascists he is bitterly opposed to the great majority taking power and favors the rule of a small minority—the capitalists. In an editorial in *Social Justice* (February 20, 1939) he stated:

> "The principle of mere 'majority-ism'—sometimes called democracy and sometimes Bolshevism—is not enough. The popular fallacy is that '50 million Frenchmen can't be wrong.' As a matter of experience and historic fact, 50 men are much more likely to be right than 50 million."

In this case Coughlin can add TEN to his fifty men and make it the SIXTY FAMILIES.

During the 1936 election campaign, Coughlin clarified his position still further in an unguarded moment. In an interview at which Dale Kramer, former national secretary of the National Farm Holiday Association, was present. Coughlin stated that *"Democracy is doomed"* and *"I take the road to fascism."* (*Coughlin, Lemke and the Union Party*, by Dale Kramer.)

**Coughlin opposes Social Security**

Yes, Coughlin is thoroughly devoted to capitalism. He opposes capitalism granting even the slightest concession to labor.

To guarantee food and clothing to a laboring man and his family when some sordid capitalist throws him out of a job would threaten the capitalist structure Father Coughlin thinks!

> "Studying it (the Social Security Act) closely, one discovers that basically it is socialistic in its conception and aims. It is socialism of the old school; socialism that offers a remedy more disastrous than the threatened evil; socialism that demands we take from those who have and give to those who have not." (*Social Justice*, October 17, 1938.)

In the same editorial he advocates giving everyone an "annual living wage" *instead* of Social Security.

What Father Coughlin considers an "annual living wage" in dollars he does not state. It must be less than social security to gain his approval!

And what would be wrong with giving a *decent* annual living wage (not less than $2,500 at present cost of living) *and* Social Security? A labor government could easily obtain that as a minimum for the workers in the richest land on the face of the earth.

**Coughlin favors regimentation of labor**

The industrial barons have long been struggling to enact changes into the Wagner Act which would benefit them. Coughlin backs up the changes they want. There must be *"no conflict"* between labor and the employers, Coughlin says. *"National unity"* is what he wants.

> "Make the United States Department of Labor a real power. Let it take over the

functions of collective bargaining—the functions which the American Federation of Labor is now trying to fulfill. Let it supplant the A. F. of L. entirely." (Interview published in the *Detroit Times*, October 10, 1934.)

Does this sound like giving labor the right to organize? What Coughlin advocates in the quotation above is exactly what Mussolini and Hitler advocated and *what they put into effect.*

Concentration camps, forced labor, prisons, starvation, endless hours of labor—this is what Father Coughlin's plan means.

### Father Coughlin favors war

Father Coughlin claims that he is opposed to war. But close attention to his words shows that he is opposed only to war against Germany and Italy *at the present time.* And even on this point he will shift quickly enough when the war actually breaks. He supported Roosevelt's war program once before. It will not be difficult for him to flop back again during the war hysteria and cry sternly over his network: *"Roosevelt's War or Ruin."*

There is no dearth of statements he has made on this point too, disclosing his *real views.*

On January 19, 1930, in the discourse entitled "Christ or the Red Fog," Coughlin attacked a Milwaukee students' conference for adopting a resolution opposing war. He condemned the students because:

> "They are unwilling to assist in building up a better navy and a stronger army to protect a country where Christ is still a King." (*Father Charles E. Coughlin*, p. 68.)

Coughlin is no less devoted to capitalism and private property than Roosevelt. He too wants a big navy and a big army. He too wants unemployed youth marching behind bayonets.

### The fine art of Jew-baiting

So incensed are the American workers at the unparalleled brutality with which Hitler has persecuted the Jews, and so great has been the wave of sympathy for them that Coughlin has attempted to deny that he is a Jew-baiter.

"We disavow all participation with those who hate Jews because they are Jews. . . ." (*Social Justice*, May 1 1939.) "If and when anti-Semitism shows its ugly head here, I shall be the first, without hope of receiving reward to condemn it both by voice and deed." Reprinted in *Social Justice*, May 1, 1939.)

But a fascist movement if it is to be successful must have a scapegoat on whom the frenzied masses can vent their rage in place of the capitalists who deserve it. (Naturally the capitalists pay well for this service.) And so Coughlin too must have a scapegoat. Coughlin like Hitler and Mussolini has selected the Jew for his scapegoat.

In order to maintain that he is not anti-Semitic, he divides Jews into two categories. Five per cent of them are *religious,* he postulates. This five per cent he favors—and if they are ever persecuted, he declares, you will find him in their front ranks! The other ninety-five per cent, he says, are *not religious.* They are communists, socialists, atheists, international bankers, and dealers in gold. In fact Father Coughlin does not pause at words far more lurid than these in marking the Jews for victims on the reeking altar of capitalism.

At the very height of Hitler's persecution of the Jews, when the whole world watched horrified, and even reactionaries scurried to place themselves on record as opposing this persecution, Father Coughlin defended Hitler's bloody pogrom and attacked the Jewish victims. (Radio speech, November 20, 1938.)

*Social Justice* from one end to the other is crammed with insinuations and innuendoes attacking the Jews. In issue after issue, Coughlin published the infamous "Protocol of the Elders of Zion," which was proved a vile forgery years ago.

In the December 19, 1938 issue of *Social Justice,* Coughlin attempted with the following lurid allegation to blacken the Chinese who have been defending themselves against the attack of Japanese imperialism:

> "Abraham Cohen, who has been variously known as General Ma and General Moi Sha, is the power behind the Nationalist government."

Even if it were true, there would be nothing wrong in a Jew fighting with the Chinese against the oppressing Japanese armies. But not even Japanese propaganda claims that such a person exists.

Outside his editorial page, Coughlin does not pay the slightest attention to differentiating the religious Jews from the ones HE *thinks* are non-religious. They are ALL *Jews* in the news articles.

For example, in the issue of *Social Justice* for June 5, 1939 he attacks Leslie Hore Belisha as "the only *Jewish* member of the British cabinet." (Who certainly as Minister of War is devoted to capitalism, and cannot be dubbed a "communist" by the wildest stretch of the term.)

> "Dissatisfaction within the British Army over the fact that England's military arm is led by a Jew, fed by a Jew, and now clad by a Jew, despite severe censorship to hush up the matter," the article asserts.

In his fantastic efforts to prove that there is an "international plot of Jewry" to enslave the world, Coughlin stops at no lie or distortion of the truth. That is one of the things he must accomplish: construct a hook-nosed wolf with golden fangs and label it JEW, if he is to succeed in becoming Fascist Dictator of America.

With all the deliberate intent of a fascist demagogue who knows exactly what he is about, Coughlin has charted the moves which he hopes will bring him to power.

What does Father Coughlin hope to accomplish by his Jew-baiting?

Split the labor movement into warring camps.

Hack and chop these camps into splintered bits.

Grind these bits into dust.

That is the purpose of Jew-baiting.

First the Jews, then the militants, then the trade-unions, each in turn will be sucked into the ravenous maw of American fascism; each of them tagged: "agent of international Socialist Jewry."

That is the purpose of Jew-baiting!

## Coughlin supports his fellow fascists

In an editorial in the January 2, 1939, issue of *Social Justice* Father Coughlin attacked a proposal that the Red Cross ship wheat for distribution to starving victims of the civil war in Spain, both Loyalists and Fascists.

He gave as his reason that since there was greater need in the territory then held by the Loyalists, most of the wheat would go to feed starving Loyalists.

When five hundred thousand refugees began pouring into France, fleeing from the advance of fascist warlord Franco after being betrayed by Loyalist army leaders who had been put into power and supported by Stalin's Communist Party and the Social Democrats, Coughlin cynically declared:

> "The hordes clamoring for escape at the border are not Spaniards. Thousands upon thousands are Russian reds." (*Social Justice*, February 13, 1939.)

Coughlin approved Hitler's seizure of Austria.

Coughlin approved Hitler's seizure of the Sudetenland.

Coughlin approved Hitler's seizure of Czechoslovakia.

Coughlin approved Hitler's seizure of Memel.

Coughlin approves Hitler's bristling war threats.

In his broadcast of March 24, 1935, Coughlin declared: *"Today the outposts of Germany are the frontiers of our civilization."*

When the work week was lengthened arbitrarily by decree in France, Father Coughlin hailed the act.

In the Far East Coughlin supports Japan and describes this militaristic dictatorship where all civil liberties have been suppressed in blood for years, as "the sole barrier against the menace of communism in the Far East." The "victory of China," he assures the reader, "would mean victory for communism in China." (*Social Justice*, December 19, 1938. See also the issues of December 26, 1938 and March 6, 1939.)

When Mussolini invaded Ethiopia (a Christian nation incidentally) Coughlin broadcast a speech attacking the Ethiopians and justifying Mussolini's criminal war. (*A Series of Lectures on Social Justice,* April 1936, by Rev. Charles E. Coughlin, pp. 17–19.)

Coughlin applauded Mussolini's seizure of Albania, calling it a "rescue," for the "benefit" of its million inhabitants.

*Why is Father Coughlin so enthusiastic about the foreign fascists?*

Let it be understood once and for all, that Father Coughlin is not an *agent* of the European dictators. Far from it. He is their *disciple* and *admirer*. But on the day that war breaks out between the United States and any one of these nations which Coughlin now lauds, he will turn against that nation as savagely as a cannibal on his aged grandfather.

What Coughlin desires is that the *methods* and the *ideology* of these fascist plunderers *sink deeply into the minds of his followers.*

Coughlin wants to organize a state *similar* to the Nazi and the fascist—*a corporate state,* and the REAL masters of that corporate state, the masters to whom he swears devotion and whose interests he represents, are *America's* parasitic SIXTY FAMILIES.

**The fascists hail Coughlin**

When the Socialist Workers Party led 50,000 demonstraters in protest against the February 20 meeting of the German-American Bund in Madison Square Garden, the 18,000 members of the Bund, meeting under protection of the biggest concentration of police in New York history, were heiling Fuehrer Fritz Kuhn, Fuehrer Hitler, and Il Duce Mussolini. But the biggest ovation of the evening, next only to that accorded La Guardia's police, was the ovation given Father Coughlin.

*Significant that the German-American Bund followers of Hitler should be so enthusiastic over Coughlin!*

An Associated Press dispatch from Rome on January 17, 1939, stated that the radio priest "received fascist praise and thanks today from the *Regime Fascista,* the newspaper that has led attacks on the Vatican in the dispute over the Italian anti-Semitic measures."

In a Berlin dispatch dated November 27, 1938, Otto D. Tolischus reports in the *New York Times:*

> "The German hero in America for the moment is the Rev. Charles E. Coughlin because of his radio speech representing National-Socialism (Nazism) as a defensive front against Bolshevism."

The *acknowledged* advocates of fascism in America are not less enthusiastic.

George E. Deatherage, leader of the Knights of the White Camellia, who insists that fascism as a movement began in America with the Ku Klux Klan long before it was copied by the Nazis, declares:

> "He is not the leader we are looking for, but America has produced no greater voice: and when the time for the showdown comes, Father Coughlin will have behind him and us, ten million mobilized followers." (*Saturday Evening Post*, May 27, 1939.)

William Dudley Pelley, Fuehrer of the Silver Shirts, another mysteriously financed "Christian" who openly proclaims his desire to Hitlerize the United States, declared in the November 14, 1938, issue of his magazine, *Liberation*:

> "This past week the aggressive Father Coughlin went on the air over a New York radio station and delivered what amounted to the prize Silver Shirt speech of the year."

It is not difficult to understand the brotherly love between the openly acknowledged fascists and the "radio priest" who has risen so rapidly from obscurity.

**Father Coughlin, speculator and stockholder**

When Coughlin was supporting Roosevelt and the New Deal during the honeymoon first term, he pronounced a series of discourses over the air on the silver question.

The burden of these speeches was, briefly, that to save the forgotten man, increase world trade, give everybody a job, and "thaw out money," it was necessary only to raise the price of silver.

> "The restoration of silver to its proper value is of Christian concern. I send you a call for the mobilization of all Christianity against the god of gold." (Quoted in the *Churchman*, June, 1939.)

Eventually Roosevelt did raise the price of silver.

And then Secretary of the Treasury, Morgenthau revealed in April 1934 that the largest holder of silver futures in the state of Michigan was *one Amy Collins, secretary to Father Coughlin.*

She held 500,000 *ounces,* costing 40 cents an ounce at the time of purchase, but purchased at 10 per cent margin, or $20,000. Every time silver went up 1 cent it meant $5,000 *profit for the holder of the* 500,000 *ounces.*

On an investment of $20,000, Coughlin made 500 PER CENT PROFIT.

It was this revelation of his silver speculations which turned Coughlin so savagely against Secretary of the Treasury Morgenthau. Even the Bund since then curses Morgenthau regularly in its ritual. Not long afterward, Coughlin switched his support from President Roosevelt to William Lemke.

In 1935 the *Detroit Free Press* revealed in a series of articles that in 1929 and 1930 Father Coughlin had speculated in stock of the Kelsey-Hayes Wheel Co. and the Packard Motor Car Co., that in one transaction alone he paid as much as $30,110.89 for Kelsey-Hayes stock and lost nearly $14,000 in another venture. The *Free Press* also revealed that Coughlin manipulated three bank accounts, one in the name of C. E. Coughlin, one in the name of the Radio League of the Little Flower, and a third in the name of Ste. Therese of the Child Jesus Parish, and that he used these funds for speculative purposes.

Father Coughlin's interest in the stock of certain automobile companies sheds an intensely illuminating light on his early ventures into the labor field.

**Father Coughlin, labor hater**

Besides having his printing done in a non-union shop, Father Coughlin constructed his million dollar Shrine of the Little Flower by hiring an open-shop contractor who paid his men 25 to 40 per cent below trade union rates. In this way Coughlin showed what he means by a "living annual wage"!

As a result, the A.F. of L. at its 1934 convention at San Francisco unanimously adopted a resolution condemning Coughlin for his anti-labor policies.

Father Coughlin favors the company union:

> "Had the motor manufacturers been in the least intelligent, they would have helped to organize a friendly and efficient union years ago." (*Eight Lectures*, p. 125.)

Father Coughlin is opposed to strikes (exactly the way Hitler and Mussolini are opposed to strikes!):

> "The National Union for Social Justice contends that strikes and lockouts are absolutely unnecessary." (Sermon, December 2, 1934.)

In 1935 a semi-company union, the Automotive Industrial Workers of America, was organized. It was known as the "Coughlin union" because of the blessing Coughlin gave it.

It was organized in order to prevent the formation of a real fighting union which would gain better conditions, better wages, and shorter hours for the workers.

But the "Coughlin union" despite its blessing, decided to strike against the intolerable conditions in the Motor Products Co. and downed tools on November 15, 1935.

In the vicious strike-breaking campaign that followed, the strikers asked Father Coughlin for help.

*He REFUSED to see their delegation.* He refused to broadcast in their behalf. He refused to speak a single word in their cause.

Let it not be forgotten, that *many of the leaders of this strike were members of Father Coughlin's organization, the National Union for Social Justice.*

The police, the armed scabs, the organized company terror—these, *combined with the Judas kiss of Father Coughlin,* broke the strike.

Yes, Coughlin promises many beautiful things to the oppressed, but when the crucial moment comes, *he is the first to plant the dagger in their backs.*

Since the formation of the C.I.O. Coughlin has assailed it venomously and incessantly.

When Governor A. B. Chandler of Kentucky ordered President Roosevelt's National Guard down to Harlan County with orders to *shoot to kill* if necessary to break the strike, Coughlin whitewashed the coal operators who have been notorious throughout the nation for half a century as one of the most tyrannical, bloody, and violent sections of the boss class.

"The Union Leaders Made Troops Necessary." (*Social Justice*, June 5, 1939, p. 21, headline to article on Harlan.)

"To guarantee the men their right to work, Governor Chandler found it necessary to call out nearly 1,000 National Guard troops to stand guard over the mines. . . . Lewis defied the forces of law and order in Harlan County, Ky., where Governor Chandler said that 75 per cent of the mine workers desired to work, despite Lewis' command that they continue in idleness. The cry of revolt (against Lewis) was heard in other sections sickened by Lewis' one-man rule over their jobs, homes, and happiness." (*Social Justice*, May 22, 1939.)

The coal operators, who are also the county officials, openly admitted that THEY *sent* for the troops to break the strike.

As a propagandist able and willing to paint up violence, terror, and intimidation of the bosses with the gentle colors of the lily, Coughlin has no equal—in America.

The Memorial Day massacre, in which Republic Steel Corporation shot down unarmed workers in the back is blamed by Father Coughlin *on the workers*. He characterizes the massacre as a "bloody riot" and asserts that it will be easy for the Republic Steel Corporation to "prove to any jury that it cost them" the $7,500,000 for which they are suing the workers they attacked. (Editorial in *Social Justice*, June 5, 1939.)

The editorial continues with a vicious attack on the C.I.O. To Father Coughlin any militant worker is a "red," a "socialist," a conspirator in the ring of "international Jewry."

When he retired "forever" from the air and public life in 1936, he returned in less than two months, January 1, 1937, with an attack on thousands of striking General Motors workers.

His civil liberties record is no better than his labor record.

In the March 13, 1939, issue of *Social Justice*, for example, he opposes anti-lynching legislation.

In the December 19, 1938, issue, he attacks the La Follette Civil Liberties Committee, which exposed the million dollar labor spy racket and the widespread use by powerful corporations of thugs, machine guns, poison gas, intimidation, terror, and violence against their workers.

Father Coughlin does not like *investigations* or *exposures* such as those conducted by the La Follette Civil Liberties Committee.

Let the fools and the suckers bite at the gaudily feathered hook Father Coughlin dangles! Labor's right to organize? Father Coughlin believes in it the same way Tom Girdler and Henry Ford and the Harlan County coal operators do. Just let the workers dare to carry a card in a genuine union! There are ways of changing those workers' minds—Memorial day Massacres, multi-million dollar damage suits, rifles and bayonets of the National Guard, a spray of machine gun slugs in the back. . . .

## Who is behind Father Coughlin?

What Father Coughlin's secret files at the Shrine of the Little Flower would reveal as to his financial backers can only be imagined.

Hitler's movement, when it was in the same stage as Father Coughlin's, was *secretly* backed by powerful financial interests—the steel magnate Thyssen and other powerful German capitalists.

Occasionally Coughlin will mention certain capitalists favorably in his radio broadcasts—Henry Ford, Walter P. Chrysler, James Rand. Father Coughlin stayed at the *San Simeon ranch of William Randolph Hearst* while on a visit to California. Mr. G. A. Richards, president of WJR is a generous financial backer mentioned by Coughlin. He mentions too in one of his broadcasts (*Father Charles E. Coughlin*, an official biography, p. 107.) the visit of Harris and LeBlanc to his shrine for intimate conversations, Robert M. Harris of the New York Cotton Exchange—a southern bourbon well-known as a cotton and silver speculator, and George LeBlanc described by Coughlin as "perhaps the world's foremost gold trader" (*an international banker!*).

The forces in Coughlin's financial background are as sinister as the forces that directed the breaking of the Little Steel Strike.

## Coughlin's program and the fascist program

Coughlin's program as it now stands bears a remarkable resemblance to the programs of fascism and Nazism when they were at a similar stage.

Coughlin appeals to the dissatisfied and restless

unemployed workers and youth, and the farmers and small merchants who are facing bankruptcy.

Hitler directed his appeals to the same sections of the population.

Mussolini built his movement from similar ranks.

Coughlin, like his predecessors proposes a "just and living annual wage," "cost of production plus a fair profit to the farmer," etc. He attacks democratic capitalism just as Mussolini and Hitler did, and attacks it contemptuously.

He proposes "revolution" as they did, the use of force. He attacks the failure of the New Deal to solve unemployment. He attacks its war program.

Coughlin is attempting to divert these revolutionary layers of the oppressed masses, just as Mussolini and Hitler before him did, from striking at the very heart and core of the *system* that produces unemployment. He turns their rage against the "international bankers," the "Jews," the "money system." He proposes economic reforms chiefly in the realms of *banking and currency.* In this way, like Mussolini and Hitler, he attempts to dissipate the revolutionary energy of the masses against bundles of painted straw.

To the capitalists he makes clear exactly where he stands by expressing his devotion to capitalism and the private ownership of property. For certain public necessities and natural resources he advocates *nationalization*; but he *emphasizes* that he doesn't want nationalization of industry.

Some of Hitler's most prominent demands make interesting reading beside Coughlin's. The Nazi platform for instance called for "abolition of the domination of interest," "the complete confiscation of all war profits," and "participation in the profits of large concerns."

*These demands, of course, were NEVER carried out.*

> "Practically all the sixteen principles of social justice are being put into practice in Italy and Germany." (*Social Justice*, February 13, 1939, p. 7.)

Let that statement of Coughlin's burn like fire on your memory!

And we might remind the lieutenants of Father Coughlin, that the secondary leaders in Hitler's organization who insisted on carrying out the Nazi program were *"purged" in a ghastly blood bath.*

When fascism marches into power it smashes the trade unions, arrests the regularly-elected leaders and appoints fascist chiefs in their place who *dictate* the new rules and regulations. They confiscate the union treasury.

They confiscate the savings accounts and the insurance of the workers, if they have any.

They build barbed wire concentration camps and herd the unemployed inside at bayonet point.

They spread the industrial spy system throughout every city, town, and hamlet of the entire nation and intensify its grip a thousandfold.

Libraries are burned. Schools are shut down. Hours are lengthened. Wages are slashed. The speed-up is whipped up to new heights. Terror and torture are turned loose. The streets flow with blood. Strikes are punished with death. Racial minorities such as the Jews and the Negroes are nailed to the cross.

Fascism is hell for the workers and the unemployed. But it saves the profits of the small handful of capitalists who control the nation's wealth. And some obscure figure becomes the all-powerful dictator of the nation's fate.

To many good-hearted people it seems impossible that fascism could come to the United States.

But it is impossible to wish away 17,000,000 unemployed.

It is impossible to wish away the dizzy downward plunge of the rate of capitalist profit since 1929.

And it is impossible to wish away the stormtroopers being trained by fascist organizations right now in America.

In city after city, the fascist movement is spreading. Trained squads of Coughlinites, protected by the police, sell *Social Justice* in the busiest streets of every city, in workers' sections, in predominantly Jewish and Negro sections.

*Fights between workers and fascists break out almost every day.*

### Can Roosevelt stop fascism?

Father Coughlin is not alone among the representatives of Big Business who hears death's knuckles rapping at the door of democratic capitalism.

President Roosevelt, nearing the end of his second term in the White House sees his New Deal collapsing like a house of cards built from an old and very dirty deck.

Only WAR can save Roosevelt—and then only for the briefest of periods.

But for this brief period he will pay the price of millions of lives of the workers, the farmers, the youth. That is why he is buying battleships with the relief funds of the unemployed.

That is why he has poured money without precedent into a war machine that outstaggers anything in the history of the country. He hopes to divert the attention of the desperate masses from *their* plight to a *foreign enemy.*

But even war is a temporary and unpopular expedient. The unemployed don't want bayonets. They want food and jobs. Roosevelt's war can only whip their fury to new heights. Father Coughlin knows all this very well. He has read a lot of fan mail since 1926.

He knows too that Big Business in its way is as desperate as the unemployed. Big Business fears the revolutionary might of the unemployed. It wants to preserve its clutches on national wealth. It wants to preserve the profit system.

Roosevelt's usefulness as a stop-gap for Big Business is almost at an end.

Roosevelt is capitalism's smiles and promises of last year.

Now the Sixty Families need a new demagogue with less smile and more promises.

General Smedley Butler has revealed that the Morgan-DuPont interests were ready to spend $3,000,000 with a promise of $300,000,000 more if necessary to finance a fascist army that would march on Washington behind the General.

General Butler turned the offer down. *Perhaps someone else did not turn that offer down.*

### Can the trade unions alone stop fascism?

The trade unions, bogged down with the bureaucracies headed by John L. Lewis and William Green, stand helpless before the terrible problems now facing the working class, the half-ruined farmers, the small business men, and the destitute unemployed.

The trade unions as fighting organizations of the working class won huge successes in the past, conquering many of the rights of labor and defending them during the upswing of capitalism. Today under the domination of Lewis and Green the trade unions if left *alone* and *without help* face disaster.

Father Coughlin understands the limitless strength of America's laboring people far better than do Lewis and Green with their corner grocery outlook.

That is why he attempts to turn the unemployed, tooth and nail, upon those organized in trade unions.

That is why he denounces the C.I.O. and the A. F. of L. over his radio network. That is why he calls strikers "idlers," and speaks of the "jobs they have left."

That is why he calls every militant trade unionist a "communist," a "socialist," a "Jew."

That is why he exerts every ounce of his voice and his pen to build up a terrible hate for the words: *communist, socialist, Jew*.

The trade unions *alone,* especially as they have been caught in the death grip which democratic capitalism has clamped upon Lewis and Green, cannot meet the situation.

A new force is needed and needed badly.

A new weapon of the working class must be forged.

An Independent Labor Party, a fighting militant political party of the working class charged with vision, with daring, with invincible *boldness* must be organized as the battering ram that will smash this entire trashy structure of New Deal politics and the poisonous fascist growths that swell upward from its rotting foundation.

### Fascism in America must be stopped!

We must not repeat the mistakes of the labor movement in Italy and in Germany which permitted forgers, sidewalk spielers, and sideshow adventurers like Mussolini and Hitler to take over power.

The first lesson to learn is not difficult: LABOR MUST DEPEND ON ITS OWN STRENGTH.

Labor must have its own independent political party.

Labor must have its own defense guards.

The greatest danger of all is to depend on the Roosevelts, the LaGuardias, the police, and the boot lickers of these former bosom friends of

Coughlin and his ilk.

The first task that labor must perform in stopping the fascist movement in America is the organization of a *workers' defense guard.*

Every union local should begin the immediate organization of a guard to protect itself from the certain onslaught of the fascists in the near future.

The sooner these guards are organized the more efficient they will become in protecting the labor movement.

Trained, disciplined, and bold *workers' defense guards* are the ONLY FORCE that can physically *stop* the fascists from overpowering the labor movement in America.

**The final answer to Coughlin**

Democratic capitalism is doomed in the United States.

It can offer nothing but war, unemployment, misery, death.

In its desperate dying struggles capitalism will attempt anything to survive.

That *"anything"* is *fascism.*

The whole fascist movement is built upon the collapse of "democracy" and complete scorn and rejection of democratic institutions, except where they can be utilized to further fascism.

The entire working class, employed and unemployed, youth and aged, and their brothers who toil on the farms, must unite in common struggle to throw out the present government which represents the capitalists and place in power a government that will *represent the workers and the farmers.*

First step in placing labor's own government in power is to organize labor's OWN POLITICAL PARTY.

Every worker must begin *thinking* INDEPENDENT LABOR PARTY, *talking* INDEPENDENT LABOR PARTY, *organizing* INDEPENDENT LABOR PARTY.

This must be done immediately.

There is not a moment to lose.

ORGANIZE AN INDEPENDENT LABOR PARTY.

**The socialist order of plenty**

Democratic capitalism is doomed.

Although it loaded them with chains and branded them with irons, even a slave state could feed and clothe its slaves. But democratic capitalism can provide neither jobs nor food for those who toil.

It deserves no other fate but to be crushed by socialist revolution.

Clean away the rubbish of democratic capitalism!

GOOD RIDDANCE!

The productive system is ready to pour out fabulous riches.

Open up the vaults and the granaries!

Open up the bursting warehouses for every working member of society!

Harvest and distribute the crops that ripen in the fields!

Open the idle factories and man the machines that will produce undreamed quantities of wealth!

An end to the blind alley of despair in America!

Fight with the Socialist Workers Party for the SOCIALIST ORDER OF PLENTY!

# SECTION TWO

*Mayor Frank Hague of Jersey City, New Jersey*

Frank Hague began his political career in 1922 in the Hudson County, New Jersey, sheriff's office which includes Jersey City in its jurisdiction. By 1927 he had become the undisputed boss of the New Jersey Democratic Party and was elected mayor of Jersey City.

With the rise of the CIO, Hague turned to fascist methods to prevent union organizing in Jersey City. Combining political pressure with ultrapatriotic, anticommunist demagogy, Hague mobilized mobs of cops, city employees, special deputies, war veterans, and others to smash union and socialist meetings. Attempts by congressmen to speak out in support of civil liberties in Jersey City were similarly crushed.

Politicians and businessmen who were determined to resist organized labor to the finish began to look to Hague's regime as an example of how to deal with social unrest. Observing the evolution of Hague from exile in Mexico, Trotsky concluded that Hague represented an incipient form of American fascism.

The beginning of World War II and the end of the depression led Hague to make his peace with the prowar leaders of the CIO. His regime shed its fascist characteristics as Hague returned to the methods of a typical corrupt machine boss. Hague retired as mayor in 1947 and died in 1956.

# 1. BOSS HAGUE'S POLICE KIDNAP NORMAN THOMAS

The Jersey City police committed a typical act of violence during the May Days by brutally assaulting, kidnapping, and deporting Norman Thomas when he attempted to speak in Journal Square on Saturday night, April 30, against Boss Hague's personal dictatorship.

The leader of the Socialist Party declared that at least half a dozen people in the crowd had been struck on the base of the neck from the rear by police nightsticks, a blow which paralyzes without leaving a mark. Among them was Louis Freader, Hoboken Secretary of the Workers Defense League. The secretary of the League, Morris Milgram, said that at least fifteen persons had been expelled from the city with Thomas, including residents of Jersey City.

### Vicious assaults

One of them was Ashley Garrick, Jersey City lawyer whose arms, according to eye-witnesses, were held by two cops while a detective punched his face so brutally that he had to be treated by a physician.

So frenzied was the melee around the seizure of Norman Thomas that the uniformed men failed to recognize the plainclothes cops of their own force. As a result one uniformed patrolman struck a detective.

The Jersey City police chief declared that Thomas had been put out of the city "for his own personal safety." Safety, presumably, against even more serious manhandling by Hague's guardians of law and order! Thomas himself branded the whole police report as fiction, "doubtless as false as the evidence against Jeff Burkitt," who is serving a six-month sentence for trying to make a speech on the same spot.

Thomas has demanded that the LaFollette Civil Rights Senatorial Committee investigate Hague's dictatorship, and has asked various federal authorities to intervene. But Hague has been sufficiently exposed in the eyes of the people by his own actions in the past period. What is needed is not further investigation but further action against this petty satrap and staunch pillar of the Democratic Party.

### Workers' initiative needed

The organized workers of New Jersey should take the initiative in launching a movement of self-defense against the unabated and ever more vicious attacks of Hague's gangsters-in-uniform. They can secure the sympathy and support of every militant force in the labor ranks, who are already aroused to the menace represented by Hague and his regime. The independent action of the militant and organized workers is the best way to restore their democratic rights to the people of Jersey City.

Reprinted from the May 7, 1938, issue of *Socialist Appeal*.

# 2. HAGUE'S RULE STILL AWAITS REAL CHALLENGE—FREE SPEECH FIGHT IMPERATIVE

Boss Hague, his private police force, and his army of officeholders remain in undisturbed possession of Jersey City. In the first test of strength between the Jersey autocrat and his opponents, the Mayor emerged victorious without a battle.

The widespread movement of popular protest engendered by Norman Thomas' expulsion from the city on April 30 and the continued provocation of Hague's agents during last week, fizzled out miserably when the two Congressmen Jerry J. O'Connell and John T. Bernard, who came from Washington to challenge Hague's dictatorship, failed to appear at the meeting scheduled for Journal Square last Saturday night.

For three days Hague prepared to prevent the meeting. Billboards and full-page advertisements appeared in all the Hudson County papers, jointly sponsored by the "American Federation of Labor Unions of Hudson County" and the "War Veterans Committee for Law and Order," headed by Col. Hugh Kelley, secretary to Governor Moore, calling upon Jersey City citizens to "show their Americanism" and "be present in Journal Square" on Saturday evening to repel the invaders. The leaders of the Democratic Ward Clubs, together with heads of AFL unions, rallied Hague's cohorts for the expected battle.

**Police fill square**

From noon on, the atmosphere around Journal Square was noticeably tense. Plain clothes cops and uniformed police were sprinkled throughout the place. The first act of violence occurred around one o'clock when Milton Filkner, executive director of the Jersey City Committee of Labor's Non-Partisan League, was socked in the jaw by a plain clothes dick for distributing leaflets. An Associated Press photographer who tried to snap the scene had his camera smashed. Police Chief Casey stood smiling by and allowed the assailants to escape.

By seven o'clock 350 police guarded Journal Square. Wrecking cars had dragged away all the autos parked in the vicinity. Escorted by mounted police and members of the American Legion, motor trucks carried 3,000 placards into Bergen Street with such slogans as "Reds Destroy Industry and Business but Not in Jersey City," "Civil Liberties is a Cloak for Communism," "Let All the Radicals and Red Foreigners Go Back to Russia." These were distributed among the waiting crowd of Hague henchmen. The Legionnaires bore two 20-foot streamers, one inscribed "Labor! AFL Will Never Join Hands with CIO and Communism," and the other, "Norman Thomas, Roger Baldwin and Stalin, One for All and All for One—Keep Out."

**Congressmen stay away**

All traffic was stopped by the police and the area roped off. By 8:30 over 25,000 people, including in large part WPA workers and city employees conscripted for Hague's demonstration, had gathered in Journal Square. The Legion bands and the paraders bearing placards, headed by the deputy police chief, kept the crowd in a state of excitement and tried to incite a lynch spirit in them.

Meanwhile, the two congressmen who were slated to speak at 8:30 had been corralled by the Stalinists at the headquarters of the International Labor Defense in Manhattan which had taken charge of the proposed meeting. There they stayed while the president of the ILD, the ex-Republican

Reprinted from the May 14, 1938, issue of *Socialist Appeal*.

congressman Vito Marcantonio, received telephone reports from the battleground in Journal Square.

At 10:45 Marcantonio announced that O'Connell and Bernard had finally been persuaded not to go to Jersey City. [ . . . ]

Thanks to the failure of the Stalinist leadership and their liberal congressmen to prepare in any adequate way to meet the mobilization of Hague's gang by rallying the workers of Jersey City in a counterdemonstration against them, they had no forces at their disposal and were compelled to capitulate in a cowardly manner before the threats of Hague's thugs. To avoid a repetition of this fiasco in the future, it is imperative that the organized workers of New Jersey take the initiative in creating a movement of self-defense against Hague's henchmen. The organized workers in the CIO constitute the only force capable of mobilizing the masses and generating a movement powerful enough to undermine Hague, dislodge him from power, and restore the elementary rights of free speech and public assembly in Jersey City.

# 3. HAGUE FRUSTRATES MEETING PLAN—CIO MUST TAKE LEAD IN STRUGGLE

Boss Hague's cops scored another victory when they broke up the mass meeting scheduled for Pershing Field last Friday evening, seized and deported the chief speaker, Representative O'Connell, knocked down his wife, and beat up CIO assistant regional director Sam Macri. Other officers of the Hudson County Committee for Labor Defense and Civil Rights, which called the meeting, were spotted and slugged by Hague's thugs.

Hague again mustered all his forces to crush the challenge of his adversaries. Over 500 cops and hundreds of conscripted office holders were active in the crowd of between ten and fifteen thousand milling around the field when O'Connell arrived. An American Legion band played martial music and Hague's henchmen waved American flags in order to generate the properly patriotic lynch atmosphere for the dirty work of his uniformed gangsters.

**Lynch spirit kindled**

No sooner had O'Connell signified his intention of speaking than the Hague henchmen shouted in chorus: "Kill the bum! Send the Red back to Russia! Throw him out!" Obeying these orders, the police closed in on O'Connell, separated him from his wife and friends, and marched him off the field to police headquarters. After holding him there for two hours, Police Chief Walsh and other "defenders of law and order" deported him on a train to Newark.

Walsh impudently asserted O'Connell was taken into custody to save his life. The Jersey Police Department's ability to protect even themselves from the excessive zeal of their own thugs was shown by the fact that the Chief and two other high officials were struck by cops during the melee.

After his expulsion, O'Connell had no better method of action to suggest than to announce, once again, that he intended to ask Roosevelt and Farley to intervene against the vice-chairman of the Democratic Party. This will make the hundredth appeal plea addressed to these "defenders of democracy" without any other result than a Department of Justice investigation on which, it was reported last week, no action had yet been taken.

**May block struggle**

O'Connell's proposed action indicates a danger that he will use his rehabilitated prestige for purely personal political ends to impede a real struggle against Hague or to compromise with the forces protecting him.

CIO representatives have been conducting negotiations with Hague's assistants in the Democratic Party to effect a compromise with him. The deal was blocked only because of Hague's intransigence.

The CIO workers must frustrate such attempts. No compromise with the Hudson County Hitler that will result in any abridgement of democratic or labor rights! Fight to the finish against Hagueism!

The CIO must step to the forefront and take the leadership of the forces in the fight against Hague. Several CIO officials took prominent parts in Friday's meeting. Several were victims of the cops. The CIO must meet this challenge by preparing an even mightier counter-offensive against Hague.

**CIO action needed**

In its own name, under its own auspices, and with its own speakers, the CIO should mobilize the

---

Reprinted from the June 4, 1938, issue of the *Socialist Appeal*.

anti-Hague forces in counterdemonstration. Such a mass assembly requires careful preparation to be successful. The events of last Friday underscore the necessity for the immediate creation of a labor guard to prevent Hague's cops from repeating their brutalities.

Several CIO bodies have already approved the formation of such a defense corps. This is a great step forward in the struggle against the Hudson County Hitler. Other labor organizations should follow this example.

Despite his show of strength and string of minor victories, Hague's regime is weakening. With a correct and aggressive policy the CIO can weld together the fighting force that can smash it to smithereens in short order.

# 4. HOW HAGUE RULES (abridged)
By James Raleigh

Readers of the daily press, learning for the first time of Frank Hague and his domination of all social and political activity in Jersey City, are induced in the main to conclude that the commotion over popular rights now engendered there by rebellious elements is a purely sporadic phenomenon that will die down in due course either as a result of Hague's temporary surrender to adverse public opinion or because of the people's fatigue in opposing his intrenched power.

Analysis will show this is not the case.

Briefly stated, Hague's control of the whole local government begins with the police and ends with the judiciary.

Today, ordinary people in Jersey know in advance who will "pass" civil service examinations for key jobs before they are conducted, who will be "elected" to public office before they are nominated, and who will be sent to jail for election law "violations" before they are tried.

No one of importance criticizes Hague publicly without suffering retribution. No one of influence organizes against him unless he seeks to use the organization as a blackmailing device to induce Hague to buy him out.

## Democracy in Jersey City

No one may vote against him if in the future he wishes a favor. The "secret" polling booth has no curtain to hide the mark on your ballot. In Jersey City pro-Hague citizens hand in their ballots unfolded as they leave the voting booth. Everybody kowtows to "Haguey" as he is fawningly called. Most people decide to play ball with him, even the Republicans.

Yet paradoxically this is also a weakness. For every politician wants to be a cog in Hague's machine.

Obviously Hague's political machine, no matter how well geared, can not be made big enough to carry all the disgruntled residents of the city, whose disgruntlement eventually finds strength in numbers and unity. Several years ago, Hague had already enlarged his apparatus to such an extent that it was top heavy. Those who could not get comfortable berths in it were not the only grumblers. Property-owners became dissatisfied with the ever-rising taxes needed to maintain it. The unemployed complained because no provision was made for them. And even loyal Democrats still working in local industries were becoming embittered at the inadequate and falling wages.

Into this hectic picture, on the heels of the glum-faced rugged individualist Herbert Hoover, stepped the smiling Friend of the Forgotten Man, Franklin Delano Roosevelt. Among others he came to save was Frank Hague, local despot of Jersey City.

In the early days of the gold rush to Washington, New Jersey applicants seeking to fill the thousands of new jobs both there and in New Jersey were frankly told to see their congressman. And Hague's congressmen were equally frank in telling them to see their ward-leaders back home.

## Recalcitrants removed

In Jersey City, men are removed from federal WPA jobs and pointedly told that they had voted against Hague. Only favored applicants, vouched for by Hague's district leaders, can aspire to fill these vacancies. Lawyers, who by nature of their more articulate profession are potential leaders of those

Reprinted from the June 4 and June 11, 1938, issues of *Socialist Appeal*.

discriminated against by the dwindling federal funds, are bought off by being given foreclosure work for those federal agencies that make mortgage loans on workers' homes. Theatre projects, writers' projects, sewing projects, music projects, lawyers' projects—all these New Deal palliatives are mysteriously closed to enemies of Frank Hague.

In the five years of the New Deal not one outspoken word has been uttered, not one unmistakable gesture made to show that Roosevelt was opposed to the goings-on in Jersey City under the tyranny of Hague. Only the other day in regard to the deportation from Jersey City of Norman Thomas and the intimidation of Representatives O'Connell and Bernard, the president announced that Hague's denial of constitutional rights was purely a local police matter. But then Hague is a vice-chairman of the Democratic National Committee.

### Roosevelt needs Hague

One hand washes the other. Without Hague to dispense WPA jobs to make voters obligated to the Democratic Party, Roosevelt could not have carried New Jersey. Without Roosevelt to delegate New Deal appointments to him, Hague could not have maintained his political primacy in New Jersey. But the signposts point to trouble. The new recession has come upon New Jersey no less than upon Illinois and Ohio. Rent checks for Jersey City people suddenly fell two months in arrears, and funds for current relief could be raised only by diverting road funds from gasoline taxes. Young boys and girls are unable to find jobs.

One result of this development was the last local election. A group of unsatisfied youths, under the leadership of 24-year-old John R. Longo, a muddle-headed Democrat impelled simply by the need of a job, saw a solution for themselves by filing a ticket in the Democratic Party primaries against Hague's hand-picked slate of candidates. Longo's naivete and inexperience, however, made him blunder in preparing his petition: He forgot to witness all the signers as they made their signatures. His petition was "thrown out" by Hague's county clerk. His political blackmail failed. Longo was tried for election law "violations," the first such case in New Jersey, although such "irregularities" are regular, even in Hague's own petitions.

The Jury was packed and the jurors even lied as to their occupations and connection in order to be sure to get on the jury to serve Hague. Longo now faces a five-year sentence for a "technical" crime as a lesson to the public on the sanctity of the ballot.

### Hopeless courses

Any attempt to end Hagueism by resort to the traditional political parties is hopeless. Hague, a Democrat, has insinuated himself into the Republican party and by patronage has tamed all potential opposition from that source. The Hague-Hoffman Democratic-Republican alliance in the last governorship term was an open scandal.

As to a rebellion against Hague by a fusion party or by a group within his own party, this is impossible so long as Hague has control over the election apparatus. In tabulating the votes, whether Republican, Democratic, or otherwise, Hague employs his own unique method of counting. By manipulating totals in Jersey City and in the remainder of Hudson County, really one continuous city, Hague arranges for a vote big enough to carry the whole state, normally Republican.

Next, Jersey City is 70 percent Roman Catholic and the church loyally supported Hague, even before he gave a $50,000 donation to the parish. Now priests in the confessional box deem it proper to ask parishioners if they voted for Hague. Of course, when Hague hollers "communism" at his opponents, the priests respond: "Communism seeks to destroy the Church."

An ouster of the Jersey City dictator as a result of church pressure is less than likely. Yet very significant is an incident of last year, in the very midst of Hague's initial fight against the CIO "drive" in Jersey City. Although the CIO was promptly painted "red" and by implication anti-Catholic, nevertheless a group of underpaid Catholic grave-diggers entered upon a sitdown strike. Needless to say, it was hastily settled and hushed up. This event shows that the worker will not always be fooled by an institution, political or religious, when it comes to their own immediate material welfare. Obeisance to a church which dwells on the "hereafter" will decrease directly as participation in a labor union which caters to the workers' well-being increases.

The only force capable of eliminating Hagueism from Jersey City or his equivalent from any other locality is the working class. Meanwhile the workers continue to be split by groupings that do them no good. They divide politically between Republican and Democratic parties to maintain a sham two-party system, which in reality is not even a one-party system but a one-man system. Many of them observe economic group distinctions within their own ranks, a bias against the CIO.

**No real conflict**

The fact is that until this date the two types of unions have not conflicted in Jersey City except in Hague's mind. No effort has been made by the CIO, the newcomer of the two, to raid either the workers or the industrial field of the AF of L. Nevertheless, the AF of L leaders in general have evinced a marked hostility to the CIO's attempt to unionize the unorganized. This enmity always arises concurrently with Hague's animosity, and invariably the AF of L's condemnation is accompanied by a lavish endorsement of "our mayor, staunch friend of labor."

The labor spokesmen behind these declarations of loyalty and confidence are frequently men who in the past have fought and denounced Hague in the fiercest terms. Today they make dictated speeches and sign prepared statements in his praise without even reading them beforehand.

Why Hague and the AF of L are so vigilant in "protecting" Jersey City from the "radical" CIO is a question of great importance. To begin with, the rank and file as well as the leadership of the AF of L have been in years past victimized and intimidated. Now they are completely regimented by Hague.

**Receivership weapon**

This was accomplished chiefly through receivership suits against a number of union locals. First, the vicious patronage system was extended to the trade unions by the appointment of Hague receivers and attorneys whose large fees liquidated the unions' funds. Second the unions were rendered impotent and useless as far as declaring or carrying on strikes was concerned. Third, local business rallied to the boss's moral—and financial—support to prevent strikes in their plants.

Fourth, the union leaders now hold their posts, not by the grace of their membership, but by indulgence of Hague. Any move in the ranks toward independence is promptly suppressed by the bureaucrats—lest the union be thrown into receivership and thus lose the last vestige of "organization." Such receivership is easily effected in New Jersey, simply by having a few members sign affidavits that the union funds are being squandered, or that the union is insolvent and cannot meet its financial obligations, or that other "equitable" grounds for receivership exist.

Then, it may be asked, why doesn't Hague permit the CIO to come into Jersey City and organize, and as soon as that is done hold the same club over its head—the threat of receivership? The answer is that if the CIO does organize, then to retain its membership it must extract from local industry some wage and hour benefits. These concessions cannot be granted without stimulating wider organization and at the same time alienating industry proportionately.

**Runaway shops**

Jersey City is a town of runaway shops, businesses that have fled from other cities to get the jump on their competitors by the low wages made possible by local nonunionized labor. This influx of sweatshops and homework industries has served and saved Hague in two ways—first, by giving some residents a bare minimum wage and thus removing them from the overcrowded relief rolls and so reducing the strain on city finances; second, by making vacant industrial properties tenantable once more and so restoring them to the ranks of sites that contribute the needed taxes that seem increasingly harder to collect as time passes. If the CIO is allowed to organize, the fly-by-night shops will fly again, these two benefits with them. Hague, to maintain himself, must fight any effort to further organize labor.

But this does not mean that the workers cannot be unionized. On the contrary, the field is fertile for an intelligent and energetic campaign. Jersey City's liberation from Hague depends on understanding, hard-working and honest leaders who must persistently and consistently, not cheaply and dramatically, organize both the workers and the unemployed. A healthy nucleus exists in the CIO unions which were organized earlier, such as the steel workers. Further sound material is the unemployed. Even the rank and file of the AF of L will support a serious and intelligently organized drive.

# 5. JERSEY CITY: LESSON AND WARNING

By James P. Cannon

Jersey City today is the testing ground of a struggle destined in the not too distant future to become national in scope and to dominate national affairs.

The most conscious representatives of the two main contending forces which will confront each other in the national struggle that is impending—the capitalist masters of America and the dissatisfied working masses—are closely studying the developments in Jersey City and drawing conclusions for the future.

It is safe to assume that a section of the capitalists have already come to certain tentative conclusions in favor of the Hague method of dealing with labor insurgence. It is important for the workers also to know what the brutal aggressions of Mayor Hague and his cohorts really signify.

They must know what the problem is in order to formulate the proper answer to it. Much can and much undoubtedly will be written on this subject, for it has a transcendent importance. Here I want to present an outline of opinion from the proletarian class point of view:

## The real meaning of Hagueism

Hagueism is not simply the individual aberration of an illiterate, provincial politician, as liberals, Social-Democrats, and Stalinists represent the matter. The Jersey City events signify a deliberate mobilization of reaction, backed by big industrial and financial interests, for a serious preliminary test of the workers capacity to resist fascistic repression.

It is no accident that the fight of Hague was directed from the start against the organization campaign of the C.I.O. Hagueism is a shrewdly devised *anti-labor campaign*, not a seemingly irrational interference with the formal rights of free speech, etc.

By the same token the aggressions of the Hague reaction can be seriously countered only by an organized resistance of the workers. Any other approach to the question is false and can only lead to defeat in the fight against Hagueism in New Jersey and its spread to other centers. No doubt the present attempt to suppress the C.I.O. in New Orleans draws certain inspiration and encouragement from the Jersey City success of Mayor Hague.

## C.I.O. bureaucrats debase struggle

The greatest aid to Hague's campaign has resulted from the pusillanimous conduct of the leadership of the New Jersey C.I.O. They renounced the fight on their own account and handed it over to liberal-Stalinist "civil liberties" bodies. The latter, as is their nature, debased the whole struggle to more of less meaningless court battles. Hague's plug-uglies wielded their clubs and black-jacks on the streets of Jersey City where the issue is really decided.

The high-placed comedians from Washington, who were assigned the task of restoring free speech in Hague's domain couldn't find their way to Journal Square and had no organized workers' force to protect them if they arrived. The publicity attending the intervention of Norman Thomas overshadowed one fact of paramount significance: There was no organized force of Jersey City workers prepared to defend the meeting. But a Workers' Defense Guard, the one factor so far lacking, is precisely the factor necessary for the beginning of a real fight. Only the Workers' Defense Guard, surrounded by the sympathy and support of the

---

Reprinted from the July 9, 1938, issue of *Socialist Appeal*

workers' mass organizations, can smash incipient American fascism—for that is what Hagueism is—and safeguard the workers' rights in Jersey City.

## Business interests behind Hague

The experience of the past weeks have shown that Hagueism is capable of organizing the entire apparatus of the city administration, its police and unofficial thugs, veteran's organizations, and all forces of reaction, together with a considerable section of the local population. It is likewise quite obvious that "business," which is the real beneficiary of Hague's anti-labor campaign, is solidly behind him. It is not for nothing that Jersey City's official slogan is: "Everything for Business."

Under these circumstances, it is, to say the least, quite naive to imagine that individuals coming from the outside, or a few dozen, or even a few hundred people from New York, can seriously challenge the Hague reaction on its home ground and overthrow it. On the contrary, the sad fiasco of the comic-opera congressional heroes from Washington is proof that we are dealing here with something far more serious than the incidental and irrational actions of a local führer. The failure to line up at least the local C.I.O. organizations for serious resistance, for the protection of speakers and of meetings, reduces any outside intervention in the situation to the status of a more or less meaningless sally, doomed to defeat in advance.

## Publicity stunts helped Hague

On the basis of the experiences of the past week, it can be said with certainty that all such adventuristic publicity stunts have only succeeded in playing into Hague's hands and strengthening his appeal to local prejudices against the "invasion" of outsiders. Speakers, and even groups from the outside can play an auxiliary and stimulating role in a serious struggle; provided only, however, that their intervention is based upon solid support of a section of the workers in Jersey City and that the brunt and burden of the fight is borne by organized workers and their defense squads. A serious challenge to Hagueism can only begin with a movement inside the ranks of the Jersey City trade unions for stern resistance to Hague and his hoodlums, official and unofficial. That is the lesson of Italy, Germany and Austria. Fascism fears no "scandal" and is not to be bluffed. It has to be beaten down.

It is not sufficient to denounce Hague as a violator of the Constitution and its Bill of Rights. These documents are sacred only for the dupes of capitalist propaganda, not for the real masters themselves. The workers in reality have only such rights as they are ready and able to defend with their own strength. Everything else under the subject of democratic rights is a lie. Hague, the authentic American fascist, answers all palaver with brutal force. For their part, the magnates of industry and finance, alarmed by labor's aggressiveness of the past few years, cannot fail to notice with satisfaction that all the arguments in court and all the pious sermons and editorials about the Constitution carry little weight against the fists and clubs of Hague's hoodlums. Force is the argument of the advance guard of American fascism. Woe to the workers of America if they do not learn in time to talk the same language!

## A fight of national significance

The fight against Hagueism has an extraordinary national significance insofar as it poses in all seriousness the problem of combating the beginnings of American fascism. It imposes on revolutionary militants, in the first place, the general task of widespread agitation for the formation of the workers' defense guards as the only way to combat fascism. Along with this must go thoroughgoing exposure of all illusions that people's front combinations, liberalistic wailings, and court struggles can seriously interfere with the advance of American fascism. It is necessary to explain to the workers, on the basis of European experience, that *if they do not fight fascism by their own organized defense guards, fascism will crush the labor movement.*

In Jersey City, and in New Jersey generally, the main task of those who understand the problem and want to meet it realistically is to carry on an intensive agitation along this line, and to introduce resolutions to this effect in all labor organizations both A.F. of L. and C.I.O., to which they have access. Revolutionary workers who are the only possible leaders of a fight to the finish against fascism will naturally take part, in the most energetic and courageous manner, in actual demonstrations against Hague.

**Fight cannot be delegated**

But it would be adventuristic folly for them to substitute the numerically weak forces of the vanguard for the genuine mass struggle of the workers' organizations. It is worse than folly for the workers' organizations to "delegate" their fight for labor rights, which is their fight for existence, to lawyers, grand-standing congressmen, "civil liberties experts" and the rest of the publicity seeking, windbag fraternity. This is labor's own fight. Only the workers, organized and steeled for physical combat, can stand up against fascist reaction and defeat it in New Jersey and on a national scale.

Bourgeois democracy, already obsolete in most of Europe, is also approaching its twilight in America with the decline and decay of American capitalism. The fate of America, like that of the rest of the world, will be decided in the oncoming struggle between fascism and the workers' revolution. The Jersey City events signalize the opening skirmishes of this grandiose struggle.

# 6. LEON TROTSKY ON HAGUE: EXCERPTS FROM A JUNE 7, 1938, DISCUSSION

In the last few days I read a French book written by an Italian worker about the rise of fascism in Italy. The writer is opportunistic. He was a Socialist, but it is not his conclusions which are interesting but the facts which he presents. He gives the picture of the Italian proletariat in 1920–21 especially. It was a powerful organization. They had 160 Socialist parliamentary deputies. They had more than one-third of the communities in their hands, the most important sections of Italy were in the hands of the Socialists, the center of the power of the workers. No capitalist could hire or fire without union consent and this applied to agricultural workers as well as industrial. It seemed to be 49 percent of the dictatorship of the proletariat, but the reaction of the small bourgeoisie, the demobilized officers, was terrible against this situation. Then the author tells how they organized small bands under the guidance of officers and sent them in buses in every direction. In cities of ten thousand in the hands of the Socialists thirty organized men came into the town, burned up the municipality, burned the houses, shot the leaders, imposed on them the conditions of working for capitalists, then they went elsewhere and repeated the same in hundreds and hundreds of towns, one after the other. With terrible terror and these systematic acts they totally destroyed the trade unions and thus became bosses of Italy. They were a tiny minority.

The workers declared a general strike. The fascists sent their buses and destroyed every local strike and with a small organized minority wiped out the workers' organizations. After this came elections and the workers under the terror elected the same number of deputies. They protested in parliament until it was dissolved. That is the difference between formal and actual power. All the deputies were sure that they would have power, yet this tremendous movement with its spirit of sacrifice was smashed, crushed, abolished by some ten thousand fascists, well-organized, with a spirit of sacrifice, and good military leaders.

In the United States it might be different, but the fundamental tasks are the same. I read about the tactics of Hague. It is a rehearsal of a fascist overthrow. He represents small bosses who became infuriated because the crisis deepened. He has his gang which is absolutely unconstitutional. This is very, very contagious. With the deepening of the crisis it will spread all over the country and Roosevelt who is a very good democrat will say, "Perhaps it is the only solution."

It was the same in Italy. They had a minister who invited the Socialists. The Socialists refused. He admitted the fascists. He thought he could balance them against the Socialists, but they smashed the minister too. Now I think the example of New Jersey is very important. We should utilize everything, but this especially. I will propose a special series of articles on how the fascists became victorious. We can become victorious the same way but we must have a small armed body with the support of the big body of workers. We must have the best discipline, organized workers, defense committees, otherwise we will be crushed and I believe that our comrades in the United States don't realize the importance of this question. A fascist wave can spread in two or three years and the best workers' leaders will be lynched in the worst possible way like the Negroes in the South.

---

Reprinted from *The Transitional Program for Socialist Revolution* (New York: Pathfinder, 1974). © 1974 by Pathfinder Press.

I believe that the terror in the United States will be the most terrible of all. That is why we must begin very modestly, that is with defense groups, but it should be launched immediately.

QUESTION: How do we go about launching the defense groups practically?

TROTSKY: It is very simple. Do you have a picket line in a strike? When the strike is over we say we must defend our union by making this picket line permanent.

QUESTION: Does the party itself create the defense group with its own members?

TROTSKY: The slogans of the party must be placed in quarters where we have sympathizers and workers who will defend us. But a party cannot create an independent defense organization. The task is to create such a body in the trade unions. We must have these groups of comrades with very good discipline, with good cautious leaders not easily provoked because such groups can be provoked easily. The main task for the next year would be to avoid conflicts and bloody clashes. We must reduce them to a minimum with a minority organization during strikes, during peaceful times. In order to prevent fascist meetings it is a question of the relationship of forces. We alone are not strong, but we propose a united front.

Hitler explains his success in his book. The Social Democracy was extremely powerful. To a meeting of the Social Democracy he sent a band with Rudolf Hess. He says that at the end of the meeting his thirty boys evicted all the workers and they were incapable of opposing them. Then he knew he would be victorious. The workers were only organized to pay dues. No preparation at all for other tasks. Now we must do what Hitler did except in reverse. Send forty to fifty men to dissolve the meeting. This has tremendous importance. The workers become steeled, fighting elements. They become trumpets. The petty bourgeoisie think these are serious people. Such a success! This has tremendous importance as so much of the populace is blind, backward, oppressed, they can be aroused only by success. We can only arouse the vanguard but this vanguard must then arouse the others. That is why, I repeat, it is a very important question. In Minneapolis where we have very skilled powerful comrades we can begin and show the entire country.

We mentioned in the discussion that Mr. Hague is not some stupid old man who imagines some medieval system exists in his town. He is an advance scout of the American capitalist class.

Jack London wrote a book, *The Iron Heel.* I recommend it now. It was written in 1907. At that time it seemed a terrible dream but now it is absolute reality. He gives the development of the class struggle in the United States with the capitalist class retaining power through terrible repressions. It is the picture of fascism. The ideology he gives even corresponds with Hitler. It is very interesting.

In Newark the mayor begins to imitate Hague and they are all inspired by Hague and by the big bosses. It is absolutely certain that Roosevelt will observe that now in the crisis he can do nothing with democratic means. He is not a fascist as the Stalinists claimed in 1932. But his initiative will be paralyzed. What can he do? The workers are dissatisfied. The big bosses are dissatisfied. He can only maneuver until the end of his term and then say goodbye. A third term for Roosevelt is absolutely excluded.

The imitation of the Newark mayor has tremendous importance. In two or three years you can have a powerful fascist movement of American character. What is Hague? He has nothing to do with Mussolini or Hitler, but he is an American fascist. Why is he aroused? Because the society can no longer be run by democratic means.

It would of course be impermissible to fall into hysteria. The danger of the working class being outrun by events is indisputable, but we can combat this danger only by energetic systematic development of our own activity under adequate revolutionary slogans and not by fantastic efforts to spring over our own heads.

Democracy is only the rule of big bosses. We must understand well what Lundberg showed in his book, that 60 families govern the United States. But how? By democratic means up until today. They are a small minority surrounded by middle classes, the petty bourgeoisie, workers. They must have the possibility of interesting the middle classes in this society. They must not be desperate. The same holds true for the workers. At least for the higher strata. If they are opposed they can break the revolutionary possibilities of the lower strata and this is the only way of working democracy.

The democratic regime is the most aristocratic way of ruling. It is possible only to a rich nation. Every British democrat has nine or ten slaves working in the colonies. The antique Greek society was a slave democracy. The same in a certain sense can be said of British democracy, Holland, France, Belgium. The United States has no direct colonies but they have Latin America and the whole world is a sort of colony for the United States, not to speak about appropriating the richest continent and developing without a feudal tradition. It is a historically privileged nation, but the privileged capitalist nations differ from the most "pariah" capitalist nations only from the point of view of delay. Italy, the poorest of the great capitalist nations first became fascist. Germany became second because Germany has no colonies or rich subsidiary countries and on this poor base exhausted all the possibilities and the workers could not replace the bourgeoisie. Now it is the turn of the United States even before Great Britain or France.

The duty of our party is to seize every American worker and shake him ten times so he will understand what the situation is in the United States. That is not a conjunctural crisis but a social crisis. Our party can play a very great role. What is difficult for a young party in a very thick atmosphere of previous traditions, hypocrisy, is to launch a revolutionary slogan. "It is fantastic," "not adequate in America," but it is possible that this will change by the time you launch the revolutionary slogans of our program. Somebody will laugh. But revolutionary courage is not only to be shot but to support the laughter of stupid people who are in the majority. But when one of them is beaten by Hague's gang he will think it is good to have a defense committee and his ironic attitude will change.

# SECTION THREE

## *McCarthyism*

McCarthyism was the most virulent expression of the cold-war witch-hunt period. Joseph R. McCarthy was elected to the U.S. Senate in 1946 with the support of the Communist Party and liberal organizations. In 1950, he suddenly emerged as the extreme exponent of the anticommunist witch-hunt, going far beyond the administrative witch-hunt then being carried out by the Truman administration.

He whipped up widespread middle-class and even working-class support with charges that the State Department was Communist-infiltrated, that "Communists" in high office had deliberately "lost" China, and that the American political "elite" was betraying the country to the "Communists." Coming into conflict with the top leaders of both capitalist parties and even with the U.S. Army, while spreading terror among socialists, labor militants, and liberals, McCarthy's movement clearly evinced fascist characteristics.

McCarthyism reached its peak during and immediately after the Korean war, when World War III was widely expected at any moment. With the turn away from head-on confrontation with the Soviet Union and the extension of prosperity into peacetime, McCarthy rapidly lost support and was deserted by his allies in the Republican Party. He was censured by the Senate in 1954 and died in 1957.

Today, the term "McCarthyism" is commonly used to describe all forms of the anticommunist witch-hunt of the post-World-War-Two period, as well as the incipient fascist development spearheaded by the Wisconsin senator.

# 1. McCARTHYISM: AN EDITORIAL

**1. Putting McCarthy 'in his place'**

Do you remember all the loud talk recently about how McCarthy was going to be "put in his place" at this session of Congress? He was put in his place all right. On Jan. 12, five days after the session opened, McCarthy was named to the powerful Senate Rules Committee.

This Committee determines what legislation should reach the floor of the Senate. It can and has bottled up bills distasteful to Big Business and the Southern plutocrats, like antilynching, FEPC and progressive social security legislation. It gives the green light to war appropriations, anti-labor legislation, witch-hunt measures and the like.

Another jurisdiction of the Rules Committee is over funds voted for Senatorial investigations. One of the most advertised features of the various Republican and Democratic plans to "stop McCarthy" was to put a financial squeeze on his investigating committee if he doesn't behave. Now McCarthy, by a mere request, has been placed on the very committee that wields power over committee finances. Thus he can fight for the finances he needs from the strategic position of Rules Committee member.

And because of the other crucial powers of this committee, McCarthy can broaden the power of his fascist machine in Congress. If one doesn't want to be blind, that's the first result of the Democratic-Republican "battle to stop McCarthy" at this session of Congress.

Lesson one: Every time the chiefs of the two capitalist parties declare war on McCarthy it ends up in a fiasco, with McCarthy strengthened. He takes another big step in his drive towards the White House.

There are good reasons why McCarthy thrives on the maneuvers of the Republican and Democratic anti-McCarthyites—

**2. The 'outflanking' technique**

The capitalist party politicians use two methods to fight McCarthy: (1) Steal his thunder. Outflank him from the right. Use bigger and better red-baiting than McCarthy. (2) Curb him, and if necessary crush him by the power of the party machines.

Neither of these methods work. They don't work because McCarthy is not just another reactionary politician who has fallen out with the machine. McCarthy heads an incipient fascist movement. His political machine is fundamentally independent from the two capitalist party machines—although he uses these machines for all they are worth to him.

Stealing McCarthy's thunder doesn't work as a tactic to undermine him. It was tried when the Republican high command ordered Attorney General Brownell to spy-smear ex-president Truman. McCarthy, far from being undermined and outflanked, stepped in and took over the whole show. He thrived on the maneuver.

It was tried again by Eisenhower in his super-red-baiting project of "alienizing" native-born Americans. The N.Y. Times is dead wrong in saying that by this act Eisenhower "certified publically once again his own leadership in the battle against communism." (W. H. Lawrence, Jan. 9.) All Eisenhower "certified" by his speech was a craven capitulation to McCarthy. And that's all he's been "certifying" during the whole year in office.

John O'Donnell, N.Y. Daily News hack, gives a revealing McCarthyite reaction to Eisenhower's

---

Reprinted from the January 18, 1954, issue of the *Militant*.

speech: "Joe McCarthy . . . won hands down—all the way from Ike's appearance when the President gave him the big hello with an affectionate wave of the arm, down to the thundering applause which greeted the President's request that Congress press harder on subversives, be they aliens or native-born or naturalized citizens. No wonder McCarthy and Senator Jenner wore broad grins."

Truman is always working at the "outflanking" technique, even though it "outflanks" him right into a spy-smeared corner. "The Communists I handled I put in jail," he boasted to a reporter on Jan. 8. "If anyone is convicted and sent to a penitentiary, he automatically loses his citizenship. I convicted my Communists. That's how I took care of them. I'm the only man who ever sent a Communist to jail."

McCarthy thrives on this stuff. It justifies his highly specialized and ruthless red-hunting machine. It gives momentum to his fascist movement.

Lesson two: McCarthyism cannot be defeated by those who play McCarthy's game; it cannot be outflanked from the right; it must be destroyed from the left, by a bloc of workers, farmers and minority peoples.

But if labor is to destroy McCarthyism before it is itself destroyed, it must launch a militant and united program of action—

### 3. To run or to fight?

There are two instructive examples of how labor is reacting to McCarthyism.

(1) When McCarthy opened his investigation of the "red menace" in General Electric, the United Electrical Workers Union (CIO) played right into his hands. The union leadership proclaimed its own witch-hunting record. It permitted victimizations; it ran for cover and cowered. Result? The GE system was "McCarthyized." The union-busting "loyalty" purge was officially introduced into private industry. GE's 230,000 workers are subject to dismissal for their political beliefs or refusing to turn stool pigeon for McCarthy. The union is weakened. The company has a new union-busting weapon.

(2) The Velde House Un-American Committee came to San Francisco, with the usual advance publicity about uncovering "red" control of unions, etc. The Independent Longshoremen's and Warehousemen's Union calmly served notice: One witch-hunting peep out of you against our union and we'll strike.

Velde was cautious. Did they really mean it? He tried a sly ruse. He prompted a stool-pigeon witness to speak about "red domination" of the Longshoremen's Union. The next morning the waterfront of San Francisco was shut down tight. Not an ounce of cargo moved. The Longshoremen massed thousands of pickets at the doors of the witch-hunting Velde committee. They considered it a matter of elementary union security to slap down hard on this labor-baiting McCarthyite stooge.

Result? The whole San Francisco Bay Area labor movement was aroused to new militancy and confidence in the fight against reaction. Students, professionals and workers organized large anti-Velde meetings all over the Bay Area. Velde retreated on witch hunting the Longshoremen. He cut his hearings short. The unions were strengthened. The union-busting employers were weakened.

Lesson three. Militant action by labor can beat the McCarthyites. The unions must refuse any form of cooperation with the witch-hunting committees—and back up their refusal with all the power at their command.

But militancy is only half the battle. Labor must have a correct social program—it must offer a fundamental solution to the problems of war and depression—

### 4. The struggle for the middle class

McCarthyism already shows clear signs of unfolding a demagogic social program to direct the discontent of farmers, small businessmen, and workers into fascist channels.

The fascists observe, just as the revolutionary workers do, the oncoming depression and the beginnings of a wave of mass discontent with capitalism—and they are preparing to use it. As the social crisis becomes more acute the question will be posed: who offers the solution to the crisis—the labor movement or the fascists?

If the workers' organizations don't have the answer, the fascists will utilize the rising discontent of the middle class, its disgust with the blundering labor leadership, and its frenzy at being ruined economically, to build a mass fascist movement with armed detachments and hurl them at the unions. While spouting a lot of radical-sounding demagogy they will deflect the anti-capitalist wrath of the middle class and deploy it against labor, and establish the iron-heel dictatorship of Big Capital on the smoking ruins of union halls.

McCarthy has already come out with a farm program! He blithely outbids all offers to help farmers threatened with ruin. Eisenhower speaks of 75% parity. The Democrats likewise. McCarthy is for "100% and more" parity.

McCarthy is talking of "broadening" his field of investigations. He said, "I may divide forces and run simultaneous investigations." The reason for this is the facility such diversification will provide for outlining a fascist program to meet the needs of all the discontented with wild demagogic promises—all the while spinning it around the main theme of the "communist menace."

Thus lesson four: IF Labor clings to the capitalist parties, if it fails to organize a Labor Party and adopt a deep-going program of socialist reorganization for America, the fascist demagogues will have a clear field. Only the working class, organized independently on the political field and armed with a revolutionary socialist program, can defeat fascism.

# 2. FASCISM AND THE WORKERS' MOVEMENT
By James P. Cannon

**THE MILITANT**
**March 15, 1954**

## 1. NOTES ON AMERICAN FASCISM
### (A letter to The Militant.)

Editor:

I haven't been able to disentangle myself from other preoccupations to send you any connected thoughts on McCarthyism and the probable character and perspectives of American fascism in general. The articles of Breitman are very effective arguments against people who will not recognize incipient American fascism until it obliges them by assuming the "classic" European form. What will they do if American fascism neglects or refuses to accommodate them in this respect, right up to the eve of the show down—which it may well do?

I will have something to say about the question of American fascism a little later when I get free from some other commitments. Meantime, I am in basic agreement with the campaign you are conducting and the arguments for it, especially those given in Breitman's articles. I believe these articles would make a good follow-up pamphlet to the first one.

Those who would judge specific American forms of fascism too formalistically by the European pattern, arbitrarily limit capitalist aggression against the workers' movement in two forms:

They see the democratic form by which the workers are suppressed through strictly legal measures in accordance with the law and the Constitution—such as the Taft-Hartley Law, formal indictments and prosecutions for specific violations of existing statutes, etc. All this, despite its obvious "inconvenience" to the workers' movement, is characterized as democratic.

On the other side they see the illegal, unofficial forms of violence practiced by "storm troopers" and similar shirted hooligans outside the forms of law, as in Italy and Germany. This is characterized as fascist.

But what about violence which is technically illegal and unconstitutional, but carried out nevertheless by duly constituted officials clothed with legal authority? What about such things as the breaking up of meetings and picket lines by official police and special deputies; wire tapping; inquisitions; screening and blacklisting of "subversives"; and all the rest of the intimidation and terror of the witchhunt? These procedures don't fit very well into the "democratic" formula, although their chief instruments are legally-constituted officials, supported and incited by press campaigns, radio demagogues etc.

This kind of illegal violence under the outward forms of law has a distinctive American flavor; and it is especially favored by a section of the ruling class which has very little respect for its own laws, and cares more for practical action than for theories as to how it is to be carried out. This is, in fact, an important element of the specific form which American fascism will take, as has already been indicated quite convincingly.

The depredations of Mayor Hague, who announced that "I am the law", were a manifestation of this tendency back in the late Thirties. Trotsky, by the way, considered Hague an American fascist. He described his unconstitutional assaults on free speech and free assembly, through the medium of

---

Reprinted from *Notebook of an Agitator,* by James P. Cannon (Pathfinder: New York, 1973). © 1973 by Pathfinder Press. Reprinted by permission.

*official police*, as a manifestation of incipient American fascism. I think he was right about that. If the workers stand around and wait until the labor movement is attacked directly by unofficial shirted hooligans, before they recognize the approach of American fascism, they may find their organizations broken up "legally" while they are waiting.

The truth of the matter is that American fascism, *in its own specific form*, has already a considerable army of *storm troopers* at its disposal in the persons of lawless prosecuting attorneys and official policemen who don't give a damn what the Constitution says. Incipient American fascism—already, right now—has a press and radio-television power which makes Hitler's *Angriff* look like a throwaway sheet. It has political demagogues, like McCarthy, who are different from Hitler mainly in the fact that they are clothed with official legal powers and immunity, while Hitler had to build up an independent, unofficial and at times persecuted movement without any direct support from the established press, etc.

"McCarthy is different," say the formalistic wiseacres, as if that were a help and a consolation. He is indeed different in several ways. But the most important difference is that *he starts* with a great power behind him, and operates with formal legal sanction and immunity. The right comparison to make is not of the McCarthy of today with Hitler on the verge of taking power in 1932, but rather with Hitler in the middle Twenties. The main difference we find in this comparison is that McCarthy is 'way ahead of Hitler.

Another point: the German-American Bund of the Thirties was not a characteristic manifestation of American fascism, but rather a foreign agency of Hitler's German movement. Neither is it correct to look now for the appearance of genuine American fascism in lunatic fringe outfits such as the Silver Shirts, Gerald Smith, etc. A powerful section of the American bourgeoisie, with unlimited means at their disposal are *already fascist-minded*; and they have a big foot in the Government, national and local. They feel no need at present of unofficial movements.

To the extent that such outfits will appear here or there, with the development of the social crisis, they will probably be subsumed in a broader, more powerful, adequately financed and press-supported general movement, which operates under more or less legal forms. It is far more correct, far more realistic, to see the incipient stage of American fascism in the conglomeration of "official" marauders represented by McCarthy than outside it.

**THE MILITANT**
**March 29, 1954**

## 2. PERSPECTIVES OF AMERICAN FASCISM

The campaign of the Socialist Workers Party against the ominous upsurge of McCarthyism, and its characterization of the McCarthy movement as American fascism in incipient form, has been misunderstood by some people who don't want to think, as well as by others who prefer to misunderstand us in order to misrepresent us.

Up till now we have not heard any cogent arguments against our campaign and its motivation. The most we can make out so far are some mutters and murmurs of dissent, to which we will give a preliminary answer while our critics and opponents are getting up the nerve to speak more distinctly.

One of the these muted criticisms appears in a clouded statement in one of the documents of the Pablo faction which Joe Hansen is taking apart in serial articles on another page of *The Militant*. Remarking that the Socialist Workers Party has "sounded the alarm on the fascist danger in the United States"—an accusation which cannot be denied—this document represents the campaign as a sign of our "pessimism", a conclusion which at the very best can be characterized only as a misunderstanding.

There is an obvious contradiction in this recognition of our campaign and the conclusion drawn from it. The woods are full of pessimists about the future of America in general, and about the prospects of American fascism in particular, but they are not organizing any campaigns. It is not in the nature of pessimists to do anything of that sort. Pessimism is not merely a gloomy view of evils to come, but a capitulatory reconciliation to them in advance. The real pessimists are simply keeping quiet—concerned to prolong their own grub-like existence, and hoping to adapt themselves to whatever comes by acquiescence and conformity.

The attitude of the SWP is the opposite of all that. The character of a party is not indicated by what it sees and points out but rather by what it does about it. To accuse the SWP of "sounding the alarm on the fascist danger in the U.S." is only to pay to the Party the indirect and unintended compliment of saying that it calls for a struggle against the danger. Pessimists don't sound any alarms or organize any struggles. They just run for cover. Pessimist is just another name for quitter and capitulator.

Some other critical murmurs we have heard, which have not yet found their way into print, represent our campaign as an "exaggeration" of the fascist danger and an apprehension of its imminent victory. That is another misunderstanding. To sound the alarm against the danger of fascism in the United States—and to state frankly that its victory is possible—is by no means to be taken as an admission that fascism is already in power, or close to it. Neither is it to be taken as a prophecy that fascism is destined to conquer eventually.

That will be decided in the struggle. The aim of our campaign is to "alarm" the labor movement to the reality of the danger and, from that, to the necessity of organizing the struggle on the right basis while there is yet time. The workers still have time to organize the counter-movement, but they don't have forever; and the sooner they recognize the central reality of the whole problem—that the issue will be decided in struggle—the better chance they will have to be the victors.

A fascist movement does not arise from the bad will of malicious demagogues. Neither is a radicalized labor movement created by the propaganda of revolutionists. Both are products of the incurable crisis of capitalism, which renders it unable to maintain a stable rule through the old bourgeois democratic forms. One way or another—these forms will be changed. The latent crisis, which has been artificially suppressed and disguised by war and military expenditures, promises to break out with redoubled fury in the coming period. This will spell impoverishment and misery for tens of millions of people, and it will generate an enormous discontent with the hopeless state of affairs. The unfailing result will be a widespread desire for a radical change.

This mass discontent and desire for a change can take one of two forms, or both of them at the same time.

The workers are the strongest power in modern society. If they show a resolute will to take hold of the situation and effect the necessary revolutionary change, the millions of desperate middle-class people—impoverished farmers, bankrupt small businessmen and white-collar elements—who have no independent power of their own, will follow the workers and support them in their struggle for power. This was demonstrated in the Russian Revolution of November 1917.

On the other hand, if the workers, as a result of inadequate or pusillanimous leadership, falter before their historical task, the allegiance of the middle-classes will rapidly shift to the support of the fascists and lift them into power. This alternative outcome of the social crisis was demonstrated in Italy and Germany.

How will things go in this country? The most "optimistic" way to answer that question is to tell the truth and to say once again: It will be decided in a struggle. Experience of other countries has already shown that a fascist movement and a movement of labor radicalization, which arise in the first place from the same cause, make their appearance at approximately the same time. But they don't develop at the same rate of speed. The "subjective" factor, the factor of leadership, plays a big role here.

In Italy, and later in Germany, the movement of labor radicalization had a big jump on fascism at the start. In these two countries fascism began to become a mass movement and a formidable power only after the workers had failed to carry through their revolution when they had the chance—in 1919–21 in Italy, and in Germany from 1918 to 1923. The tumultuous rise of the fascist movement in those two cases, and its eventual victory, were the answer to the workers' default and the penalty for it.

Here in the United States we see a somewhat different development of the two antagonistic forces—fascism and workers' radicalization—and a different rate of speed in their development. But these are only tentative manifestations which are not yet by any means decisive. The extraordinary thick-headedness of the labour bureaucracy in this country, and the lack of a revolutionary party with a base of mass support, have given incipient fascism the jump on the labor movement. A form of preventive fascism, of which McCarthy is indubitably the chief representative, has already got a head start and has widespread ramifications of support, inside the governmental apparatus as well as outside it. To recognize that fact is not to conjure up imaginary dangers but simply to recognize the obvious reality of the situation.

And this recognition of reality is the first prerequisite for the organization of an effective counter-movement. McCarthyism, as it appears today, is undoubtedly an *incipient* fascist movement, but that's all it is. The beginnings of a fascist movement aiming to take power in this country, and fascism already in power, are not the same thing. Between the one and the other lies a protracted period of struggle in which the issue will be finally decided. Whoever recognizes that and "sounds the alarm", and thus helps to prepare the struggle of the workers is doing what most needs to be done at the present time. Such a campaign is by no means a manifestation of pessimism, but the best antidote for it.

Power is on the side of the workers, and all the chances of victory are in their favor. But they will never gain the victory without the most resolute struggle. The first prerequisite for that is an understanding of the irreconcilable nature of the struggle and what it's all about. The fate of America, and thereby of all mankind—that's what it's all about.

**THE MILITANT**
**April 5, 1954**

### 3. FIRST PRINCIPLES IN THE STRUGGLE AGAINST FASCISM

The honorable Joseph McCarthy is not much of a thinker himself, but he has certainly stimulated a lot of thought, or what passes for it, in the minds of others. His unbridled aggressiveness in recent months has stirred up quite a fluttering in the dovecotes of so-called liberalism. The pontifical pundits, who yesterday thought the specter could be exorcised by ridicule, or by pretending not to notice it, are now deep-thinking second thoughts about the Wisconsin demagogue and what he stands for.

Some apprehension of the deadly seriousness of McCarthyism has even begun to dawn in the thick skulls of the official labor leaders, and that alone is testimony to its penetrating power. It is now widely recognized that if the Wisconsin demagogue is crazy, he is crazy like a fox, and has to be taken seriously. It would also seem that the liberals, and the labor leaders who farm out their thinking to the liberals, are catching up with the SWP, as far as the definition of McCarthyism is concerned. Lately we see more and more references to McCarthy as an American Hitler. For example, Adlai Stevenson, who cannot justly be called an extremist, referred to McCarthy in his Miami speech as the apostle of a "malign totalitarianism".

But we are still poles apart from the liberals and the labor skates on the main question; that is, the analysis of the causes of this preliminary manifestation of a "malign totalitarianism"—the Stevensonian euphemism for fascism—and the program for struggle against it. They all regard our revolutionary approach to the question as extreme and unrealistic. The unrealism, however, is on their side, because they separate McCarthyism from the social causes which have generated it, and which in fact, make such manifestations inevitable. If McCarthy did not exist American capitalism would have to invent him, or a reasonable facsimile.

In every great social struggle, those who understand its laws and foresee how it must develop according to those laws, have a big advantage over those who deal with surface manifestations. If the Socialist Workers Party had been the first and only group in American political life to state categorically that the rise of a fascist movement in the United States is an absolute certainty; and likewise the first to recognize McCarthyism as the preliminary manifestation of American fascism, and to call it by its right name—this was not guesswork in either case.

Our approach to the question of American fascism, as to every other political issue, begins with and proceeds from a basic theory of American perspectives which is different from that of all other political parties and tendencies. That is not because we deny America's exceptional position in the world today. It is known, and has been said often enough, that American capitalism is in a different position from other sectors of the same world in other countries. I am even willing to repeat it once again if such reassurance will do anybody any good But there are points of similarity as well as of difference, and the former are more important than the latter. That is the main point.

The American capitalists are richer and stronger than their counterparts in other lands. They are also younger and more ignorant, and therefore more inclined to seek a rough settlement of difficulties without diplomatic subtlety and finesse. All that does not change the fact that American capitalism operates according to the same laws as the others, is confronted with the same fundamental problems, and is headed toward the same catastrophe.

Of all the mistakes that can be made in judging the nature and prospects of the present social system in this country—and it is safe to predict that the American labor leaders, being what they are, will exhaust every possibility in this respect—the worst and most disorienting mistake is to regard American capitalism as *fundamentally* different; as immune from the operation of the same laws which determine the evolution and development of the same social system—through crisis, revolution and counter-revolution—in other countries.

This pernicious theory of "American exceptionalism", which seized the leadership of the American Communist Party in the latter days of the great boom of the Twenties, disoriented the party in the great crisis which exploded soon afterward. This same theory, which is today held by the entire labor officialdom, is what disarms the American workers at the present time more than anything else, and gives the preliminary movement of American fascism such an easy advantage in the beginning.

We Trotskyists never belonged to this school of "exceptionalism". In 1946, right at the time when the editorial spokesmen of American capitalism were proclaiming the advent of "The American Century", and the American labor leaders were adjusting their so-called thinking to this illusory prospect, the Socialist Workers Party outlined a different and more realistic perspective for this country. The "Theses on the American Revolution", adopted by the party convention in that year, expressed its conception in the very first paragraph, as follows:

"The United States, the most powerful capitalist country in history, is a component part of the world capitalist system and is subject to the same general laws. It suffers from the same incurable diseases and is destined to share the same fate. The overwhelming preponderance of American imperialism does not exempt it from the decay of world capitalism, but, on the contrary, acts to involve it ever more deeply, inextricably and hopelessly. U.S. capitalism can no more escape from the revolutionary consequences of world capitalist decay than the older European capitalist powers. The blind alley in which world capitalism has arrived, and the U.S. with it, excludes a new organic era of capitalist stabilization. The dominant world position of American imperialism now accentuates and aggravates the death agony of capitalism as a whole."

This formulation of American perspectives, which governs all the work of the Party, determines its analysis of McCarthyism as the incipient stage of American fascism; its categorical assertion that this movement will grow bigger, stronger and more cohesive with the development of the oncoming crisis; and its program for the struggle against it.

Some such manifestation as the present McCarthy movement was foreseen; and it needed only to make its appearance and score some initial successes, as it has manifestly done since the Brownell-Truman affair, for the Party to react with its counter-campaign of agitation. The fact that the party members have recognized the necessity of the campaign, and responded to it with unanimous participation, is a sign that they were prepared for it by a long previous period of doctrinal education.

I speak of our view of American fascism as a doctrine; for we consider it a matter of principle that the war prosperity of U.S. capitalism has been sick with a latent crisis from the start: and that this crisis is bound, sooner or later, to explode with devastating fury. This exploding crisis is certain to produce two antagonistic phenomena; a fascist movement on the one side, and a radicalized labor movement on the other.

The same social crisis which poses the threat of revolution in each and every capitalist country without exception, likewise generates the attempt to head off such a revolution by means which ruthlessly break down all the old forms of democratic rule. An organized fascist movement is an imperative necessity to the ruling class in every modern capitalist state threatened with social revolution; and is, in fact, a reflexive answer to it. In this view, the fascist movement is not something arbitrarily created by demagogues, to be talked-down by appeal to reason and an alliance of all men of good will. Fascism is organized counter-revolution.

There is no law which forbids such a counter-revolutionary movement to get under way before the prospect and threat of revolution is clearly evident to all. A social revolution is immanent in the present position of American capitalism, and so is the counter-revolution. McCarthyism, as the first definite preliminary manifestation of the counter-revolutionary movement, does not lose this basic characteristic simply because it is a preventive mobilization against a revolution which has not yet taken visible form.

McCarthyite fascism has its cause and origin in the crisis of a social system which is pregnant with a revolution; and is in fact, the preliminary form of a preventive counter-revolution. A general hue and cry against McCarthyism won't amount to much until this is recognized.

**THE MILITANT**
**April 12, 1954**

## 4. A NEW DECLARATION OF INDEPENDENCE

Fascism is a product of the crisis of capitalism and can be definitively disposed of only by a solution of this crisis. The fascist movement can make advances or be pushed back at one time or another in the course of this crisis; but it will always be there, in latent or active form, as long as the social causes which produce it have not been eradicated.

Looked at from this standpoint, the threat of American fascism is not a short-term problem, and by no means can it be eliminated at the next election—or, for that matter, at any other election. The American fascist movement, and the workers' struggle against it, will be a long drawn-out affair, from now to the final show down, which in the end can be nothing less than a show down between fascist capitalism and the workers' revolution.

If the default of the labor movement has given American fascism, in the incipient and preventive form represented by the McCarthy movement, an advantage at the start, it still represents nothing more than an episode in a long struggle which will have many ups and down. The real movement of American fascism is now only in its preliminary stages of formation, and the counter-movement of the workers against it is not even started yet.

At any rate, American fascism, in its McCarthyite form or under some other aegis, is bound to provoke a militant resistance from the workers as soon as it passes over from its present preoccupation with a hunt for spies and "subversives" to a direct assault on the labor movement. Thereafter, the fascist movement will not develop on a straight ascending line. There will be zigzags on one side and the other, advances and set backs and periods of stalemate. In this protracted conflict the labor movement will have time to get a clearer picture of the real nature of the problem, and to mobilize its forces for an all-out struggle.

At the present time, the myopic policy of the liberals and the labor leaders is concentrated on the congressional elections next fall, and the presidential election to follow in 1956. A Democratic victory is counted on to deal a death blow to the McCarthy aberration. "McCarthyism is becoming a danger all right, and it begins to look like a fascist movement; but all we need is a general mobilization at the polls to put the Democrats back in power." Such are the arguments we already hear from the Democratic high command, the literary liberals, the labor leaders and—skulking in the rear of the caravan, with their tails between their legs—the Stalinists.

This would really be laughable if humor were in place where deadly serious matters are concerned. The Roosevelt New Deal, under far more favorable conditions, couldn't find a way to hold back the economic crisis without a war. A Stevensonian version of the same policy, under worse conditions, could only be expected to fail more miserably. A Democratic victory might arrest the hitherto unobstructed march of McCarthyism while it re-forms its ranks. It might even bring a temporary moderation of the fury of the witch-hunt. But that's all.

The fascist movement would begin to grow again with the growth of the crisis. It would probably take on an even more militant character, if it is pushed out of the administration and compelled to develop as an unofficial movement. Under conditions of a serious crisis, an unofficial fascist movement would grow all the more stormily, to the extent that the labor movement would support the Democratic administration, and depend on it to restrain the fascists by police measures.

Such a policy, as the experience of Italy and Germany has already shown, would only paralyze the active resistance of the workers themselves, while giving the fascist gangs a virtually free rein. Moreover, by remaining tied to the Democratic administration, the labor movement would take upon itself a large part of the responsibility for the economic crisis and feed the flames of fascist demagogy around the question.

That would be something to see: The fascists howling about the crisis, and stirring up the hungry and desperate people with the most extravagant promises, while the labor leaders defend the administration. The official labor leaders are fully capable of such idiocy, as they demonstrated in the last presidential election. But with the best will in the world to help the democratic administration, they couldn't maintain such a position very long.

The workers will most probably accept the recommendation of the labor leaders to seek escape from the crisis by replacing Republican rascals by Democratic scoundrels in the next election. But when the latter become officially responsible for the administration, and prove powerless to cope with the crisis, the workers will certainly draw some conclusions from their unfortunate experiences. The deeper the crisis, and the more brutal the fascist aggression fed by the crisis, the more insistent will be the demand for a radical change of policy and a more adequate leadership.

From all indications, the workers' discontent will be concentrated, at first, in the demand for a labor party of their own. This will most probably be realized. It will not yet signify the victory over fascism—not by a long shot—but it will represent the beginning of a counter-movement which will have every chance to end in victory.

The break with the Democratic Party will be an implicit recognition that the fight against fascism is fundamentally a fight against capitalism in the period of its agonizing crisis of disintegration and decay; and that there is no hope of victory for the workers in alliance with one of the parties of this same capitalism, and still less under its leadership, as at present. The formation of a labor party, based on the trade unions, will represent the American workers' Declaration of Independence. It will be a great turning point in American history. All developments will be speeded up after that.

It would be a great mistake, however, to speak of a prospective labor party as the solution of the problem of fascism. As in 1776, the new Declaration of Independence will signify not the end, but the beginning of the real struggle. The final outcome will depend on the program and the leadership These will become the burning issues of an internal struggle for which the labor party will provide the main arena. It is from this point of view—clearly stated at all times—that we advocate the formation of a labor party and do all we can to hasten the day of its appearance.

**THE MILITANT**
**April 19, 1954**

### 5. FASCISM AND THE LABOR PARTY

Our campaign against McCarthyite fascism is an agitational campaign to arouse the labor movement to the advancing danger, and to stimulate a counter-mobilization of the workers. Along this road we participate wholeheartedly in every practical action regardless of its official auspices. Such actions have a logic of their own and can lead, in a step-by-step process, to a final settlement of accounts with fascism and the social system which turns to fascism as a last resort.

The struggle against fascism is an affair of the working class, and the revolutionists would only defeat their own purpose by sectarian abstention from anti-fascist mobilization of the class. *The Militant* is certainly correct in calling for a general congress of labor, to consider the question of a united anti-fascist struggle of the entire labor movement; and in advancing the slogan of a labor party as the general formula for the political independence of the workers in this struggle.

But even while advancing and popularizing these slogans, which sooner or later will be accepted and supported by millions, we ought to explain their limitations as well as their advantages. The assertion that the labor party "will stop Mc-

Carthyism", which makes its way into our agitation now and then, is an oversimplification which ought to be guarded against. A labor party would represent a gigantic step forward in the struggle against fascism, but is not in itself a panacea for victory.

A fascist movement is an inherent necessity to the capitalist system at a given stage of its disintegration. Nothing will "stop fascism" short of the overthrow of capitalism. This is the simple truth of the matter; and if our party doesn't tell this truth constantly it would have no reason to exist. There are plenty of others to sow confusion and foster illusions, and they are not entitled to any direct or indirect help from us. There is good ground for confidence that the workers will prevail in the final showdown, and that fascism will never come to power in America. But there is no ground for the assumption that the workers' victory will be quick and easy, or that a mere demonstration of organized labor's opposition would scare the fascist menace off the map.

The workers of Germany were politically organized in two great mass parties. Moreover, the Communist and Social Democratic parties of Germany, who shared the allegiance of almost the entire working class between them, were at least formally committed to a socialist program. They collapsed under the blows of fascism just the same, precisely because they hoped for the miracle of victory without a real struggle. That would surely happen in this country too, even with a labor party supported by the entire trade-union movement, if it should offer no more resistance to fascism than plaintive objections and parliamentary opposition.

I believe it is correct to say that a real first step toward a serious struggle against American fascism could hardly be anything less than the formation of a labor party. As long as the trade unions are allied to the Democratic Party and thereby, in effect, dependent on capitalist politicians to protect them against the onslaughts of a fascist party dedicated to a capitalist counter-revolution they have not even begun to fight.

For that reason, it is perfectly correct to put the slogan of a labor party in the center of our agitation and to concentrate all agitation around it. But in doing so, we have no need to oversimplify the fundamental problems posed by the beginnings of a fascist movement, and to think that we are doing our full duty if we stop at that. We must look far ahead—from the beginning of the struggle to the end—and keep the goal in mind in all that we do and say. We have to be with the workers in all their practical actions and in all their struggles. But we will be no help to them if we simply follow along, keep quiet about the workers' present illusions and thereby foster them.

If we see the impending struggle in its true shape as a drawn-out affair, we must recognize that coming developments will work powerfully to realize the slogans of the present. After that, new events will prepare the conditions for a widespread acceptance of the more advanced slogans required at a later stage of development. As a revolutionary party, we ought to foresee these developments and formulate the necessary slogans in advance.

Looking to the future, as measured now only in years rather than in decades or generations, it can be expected that a labor party will take shape and command the allegiance of millions of workers from the start. This will represent a real beginning of the anti-fascist mobilization of the American working class, which will just be another name for the mobilization against capitalism, of which fascism is the final resort. But our agitation, and our participation in practical actions leading to this preliminary mobilization, will have real importance and significance only to the extent that we keep the whole line of future developments in mind and prepare ourselves and others to meet them.

If the slogan of a labor party based on the trade unions is the most correct and necessary general slogan of agitation at the present time, the simultaneous explanation of the inescapable trend of developments toward a revolutionary show down, and the building of a party of conscious revolutionists based on this perspective, cannot be put aside in the meantime. The two tasks go together; and taken together, they constitute the most important work of preparation for things to come.

**THE MILITANT
April 26, 1954**

## 6. IMPLICATIONS OF THE LABOR PARTY

The formal launching of an Independent Labor Party, the indicated next step in the preliminary mobilization of the American working class against a rising fascist movement, will hit this country like a bomb exploding in all directions. It will not only blow up the traditional two-party system in this country and bring about a basic realignment in the general field of American politics. It will also mark the beginning of a great shake-up in the labor movement itself. The second result will be no less important than the first, and it should be counted on.

Under the present system the political stage is occupied by two rival capitalist parties, which in reality represent two different factions of the ruling class. The workers play merely the part of a chorus in the wings and have no speaking part on the stage. The formation of a labor party will change all that at one stroke. The struggle of capitalist factions for control of the government will be subordinated to the struggle of classes, represented by class parties. That is the real meaning of politics anyway.

The political realignment, brought about by the appearance of a labor party on the scene, cannot fail to have profound repercussions inside the labor movement. There will be a great change there too. The break of the trade-union movement with capitalist politics will coincide with the rise of the big opposition to the present official leadership. This rank-and-file opposition movement will most likely take shape in the struggle for a labor party, and be identified with it.

To imagine that the present official leaders can make the great shift from the Democratic Party to independent labor politics, and maintain their leadership smoothly in an entirely new and different situation, requires one to overlook the basic causes which will force them to make this shift. That is, the radicalization of the rank and file and their revolt against the old policy. No matter how it is formally brought about, a labor party will be the product of a radical upsurge in the ranks of the trade unionists. The more the officialdom resists the great change, the stronger will grow the sentiment for a different leadership. Even if the present leaders sponsor the labor party at the start, they will be under strong criticism for their tardiness. The real movement for a labor party, which will come from below, will begin to throw up an alternative leadership in the course of its development.

The demand for a labor party implies the demand for a more adequate leadership; and the actual formation of a labor party, under the auspices of the present official leadership, would only accelerate the struggle under more favorable conditions. As revolutionists, we advocate the formation of a labor party with this perspective also in mind.

It is true that the simple fact of the formation of labor party, by itself, would have a profound influence in speeding up radical and even revolutionary developments. But those who are satisfied with that might as well retire from the field and let the automatic process take care of everything. The automatic process will not take care of anything except to guarantee defeats. The conscious revolutionists, however few their numbers may be in the beginning, are a part of the process. Their part is to help the process along by telling the whole truth. The fight for a labor party is bound up with the fight to cleanse the labor movement of a crooked and treacherous leadership, and cannot be separated from it. Those radicals and ex-radicals who are willing to settle for a labor party, leaving the question of program and leadership unmentioned, are simply inventing a formula for their own betrayal.

It is not permissible for revolutionists to pass themselves off as mere advocates of a labor party, pure and simple, like any labor faker who devotes Sunday sermons to this idea. A labor party headed by the present official labor skates, without a program of class struggle, would be a sitting duck for American fascism. That's the truth of the matter, and advocacy of a labor party isn't worth much if it leaves this truth unsaid. Large numbers of trade-union militants know this as well as we do. They know that the present official leaders are no good for a real fight on any front, and that they have to be thrown out before there can be any serious thought of a show down with American fascism.

Those militants who know the score on this ought to organize themselves in order to conduct their struggle more effectively. This organization of the class conscious workers can only take the form of a revolutionary party. There is no substitute for that. And since the SWP is the only revolutionary party in the field, there is no substitute for the SWP. Those workers who today already recognize the necessity of a labor party ought to take the next step and unite with the SWP in its effort to direct the struggle toward a revolutionary goal.

# 3. DRAFT RESOLUTION ON THE POLITICAL SITUATION IN AMERICA (excerpt)

The following is an excerpt from the draft political resolution prepared by the Political Committee of the Socialist Workers Party prior to the December 1954 convention of the party. The excerpt is reprinted from SWP *Discussion Bulletin* A-20 in 1954. When the rapid decline of McCarthyism in the fall and winter of 1954 considerably reduced its weight in American politics, this section of the resolution was revised and shortened. The political evaluation of McCarthyism as an American form of incipient fascism was retained.

The resolution approved by the convention stated: "In its incipient stage, a fascist movement is subject to far greater ups and downs than the democratic capitalist political machines that pave the way for it. In this it reflects the shifting moods of the middle class, constituting a barometer of the intensity of the crisis and the degree of political independence of the labor movement as well as the concessions or blows it receives from the liberal opposition to fascism. This is well illustrated in the case of the McCarthy movement. From obscurity, the Wisconsin demagogue became a national figure in a few months in 1950. By the end of 1953 his movement dominated the political scene. Then within a year, after the Army-McCarthy hearings, he suffered a sharp setback. The present eclipse of McCarthy should not be regarded as a definitive defeat of native fascism. The basic cadre is not smashed; in fact it is hardened by such experiences. Moreover, the basic causes of fascism, continuing to operate, will prepare a fresh revival of the movement. In the event of a social crisis, McCarthy's movement would show a rapid resurgence.

"At the present conjuncture, however, the censure of McCarthy by the Senate—by far the most serious reverse he has sustained—signified unmistakably that the decisive sections of the ruling class are not ready to entrust their destiny to a fascist dictator. In the current policy of the ruling class, which seeks a modus vivendi with the Soviet bloc instead of a headlong course toward an early war showdown, there is no place for McCarthy—except in the corner into which he has now been thrust." (SWP *Discussion Bulletin* A-26, December 1954.)

In his report to the December 1954 convention, published in the Winter 1955 issue of *Fourth International*, Morris Stein made some criticisms of the SWP's campaign against McCarthyism in the previous period.

"The delay in the war perspective was recognized by us some time ago and we explained it publicly in articles and speeches," Stein told the convention. "What we did not do was correlate this factor with the prosperity that still holds despite considerable oscillations. These two factors—the deferment of war and the continued prosperity—preclude McCarthyism, the American form of fascism, from a feverish growth that could make it a contender for power in the immediate period before us.

"Yet it must be admitted that we tended to give a contrary impression in our otherwise excellent campaign against McCarthyism during the past year, both in the press and in the first draft of our main political resolution, drawn up some months before the election, where we still made the fight against McCarthyism the main axis of our general line. While we recognized the possibility of a check being administered to McCarthy and his movement suffering a setback, we placed so much stress on the ultimate danger of fascism that it did not appear ultimate but immediate, and we failed to grasp the full implications of the censure move as a severe tactical defeat for McCarthy."

## The political crisis

Symmetrical to the weakening of its international position, American capitalism has become increasingly malignant in its domestic politics. With the opening of the "cold war" in 1946 under Truman, American imperialism became the chief organizer of the world counterrevolution. It is not possible to revive, bolster, and sustain every reactionary force abroad, from the Japanese Mikado, Chiang Kai-shek, and Syngman Rhee in Asia to the former Nazis, Franco and the Vatican in Europe, without affecting the ideology of the home front. The antidemocratic views and moral corruption of these allies tend to become fashionable in America—all the more so in view of the losses abroad and the appearance of fresh obstacles requiring further postponement of war. The rantings of a Chiang Kai-shek or Syngman Rhee on the need for a supreme effort to reduce the anticapitalist countries to an open arena for imperialist exploitation strike a responsive chord. Their views become a factor in American politics.

And while organizing counterrevolution abroad, Big Business at home opened a reactionary drive to prepare the domestic front for World War III. American imperialism had sufficient resources in World War II to buy off the labor bureaucracy and a section of the working class, thereby blunting the opposition to war and gaining effective allies in keeping it under control. These resources are now gone. The sacrifices that would be demanded of the workers in the projected atomic conflict are of an order qualitatively different from anything demanded of the workers in the past. The ruling class does not count on buying off this opposition or seriously expect that the labor bureaucracy can contain it. Consequently they are resorting more and more to the club.

The unions are marked as the major objective, but the dollar plutocracy is not so stupid as to begin with a head-on struggle against such a force. Their strategy is "one at a time." They have carefully singled out unpopular victims to whose defense the labor movement would be least likely to rally, and given them the works first. At the same time they have moved step by step to construct a police state capable of strangling all democratic institutions and traditions and transforming the trade unions into an integral part of the police-state apparatus. The norm of democracy in America is thus disintegrating. The disintegration has gone so far that for the first time in American history a political party has been outlawed.

The beginnings of the witch hunt can be traced back to 1940 when Roosevelt signed the Smith "Gag" Act and personally gave the word to persecute the leaders of the Socialist Workers Party and Local 544 of the Teamsters. However, the need to appear as champions of democracy in the war, coupled with the support that both the labor bureaucrats and Stalinists gave the war, caused the Roosevelt administration to defer a wide-scale witch hunt.

With the fall of Japan, a new chapter opened. The administration sought to begin its drive against the labor movement by driving a wedge into it, inspiring certain labor leaders to carry the ball first.

An attempt was made as early as 1945 to use the AFL as a bludgeon against the "Communistic CIO." This was short-lived. John L. Lewis, who appeared to be spearheading this maneuver, came into conflict with the government and the rest of the AFL bureaucracy. But it was sufficient to open the witch hunt in a most important area—the unions themselves.

The Murray leadership of the CIO responded by opening a preventive witch hunt of its own in the CIO. The Stalinist trade union leaders cooperated with Murray in this in the early stages, hoping to salvage their posts and positions by going along with the relatively mild edicts of the Buffalo CIO convention in 1946 ending the autonomy of the CIO councils.

But with this infringement on trade-union democracy, the sluice gates were opened. The inner CIO witch hunt gained momentum, finally engulfing every union and resulting in the expulsion of the Stalinist-dominated internationals.

The witch hunt became the main political instrument in the drive against the democratic form of government. This was accompanied by administrative orders and a wave of federal and local antilabor legislation beginning with the Taft-Hartley Act in 1946, all of which was aimed at shackling the unions and reducing the Bill of Rights to a scrap of paper.

In the country as a whole, Truman's so-called "loyalty" order of 1947—the domestic parallel to the launching of the "cold war" abroad—gave enormous impetus to the witch hunt. From the government, the hunt for "reds" spread to the waterfront and to industries engaged in production of war materiel, and from there to industry as a whole. The purge swept Hollywood, radio, TV, the schools, and the churches. The government bureaucracy itself became a major hunting ground as the hysteria over the "red" danger charged the national atmosphere.

But a witch hunt has a logic of its own. It can be kept going only by providing fresh sensations, each more startling than the last. Otherwise it tends to die down. Since the witch hunt is an essential element of the drive to psychologize the people for war and for smashing the unions, Big Business cannot permit it to die down. And so the fresh sensations are provided. America is even given the electrocution of "spies."

At a certain point, however, the fantastic premises of the witch hunt begin to appear to be true, especially to a nervous middle class. A desire thereupon arises in this section of the population for a drastic solution to the obsessing fear. Each new sensation, proving the "correctness" of the new outlook on reality, deepens this need. The witch hunt thus becomes ready for a qualitative change. Or to put it in different terms, the witch hunt becomes ready for division, the birth of something new.

In 1950 the first major signs of a qualitatively different kind of witch hunt appeared when Senator McCarthy made his notorious speech at the Wheeling, West Virginia, Republican Women's Club attacking the U.S. State Department of softness over "Communist infiltration." The appearance of the obscure Wisconsin demagogue on the national scene was noted by us at the time as the possible beginning of a "super witch hunt." The atmosphere in which the speech was delivered was "made to order," we said, "for the rise of a fascist movement that can quickly overtake traditional politics in the United States."

Since that time the witch-hunt drive has shown increasing signs of splitting into two fundamental segments—the witch hunt of the capitalist regime as such which develops organically so to speak from the old structure of bourgeois democracy towards a police state, and the witch hunt led by McCarthy that has as its fundamental aim replacing the bourgeois democratic structure with a fascist regime founded on the destruction of the old democratic institutions and above all the destruction of the trade unions as independent working-class organizations.

In November 1953 this development was dramatically projected on the national arena when McCarthy in a radio-TV speech answered ex-president Harry Truman. Brownell's smear of Truman as the protector of Harry Dexter White, an alleged Russian agent occupying a high government position, had been properly characterized by Truman as "McCarthyism." After Truman's rebuttal, McCarthy took over, hurling his challenge November 24 at both the Democrats and Eisenhower Republicans and clearly delineating the independent fascist course of his faction for the 1954 elections.

These fireworks illuminated the whole national political scene, showing the emergence of a fascist nucleus in the administration and in the Republican Party and the crystallization of an incipient fascist movement in the United States.

As McCarthy predicted at the time, "communism," or to speak more accurately, the formidable growth of his fascist movement, became the key issue in the 1954 elections. The development of McCarthyism has placed a question mark over the continued existence of every democratic institution in America, including not only the unions, but all political parties outside of McCarthy's faction. The death agony of the capitalist system, having caught up with the United States, finds its symptoms most glaringly displayed in the form of an acute political crisis from which no one, Republicans, Democrats, labor bureaucrats or any one else can escape. McCarthy is forcing America to confront its great historical alternative—fascism or socialism.

## Our analysis of McCarthyism

In response to the emergence of McCarthyism in November 1953 as a dominant issue in American politics, the Political Committee of the Socialist Workers Party developed an analysis and program of action for struggle against this fascist menace. The main points of the analysis are as follows:

The election of Eisenhower was a result of the prolonged refusal of the labor bureaucracy to lead the working class on to the road of independent political action and—in the absence of any political threat from the labor bureaucracy—the determination of Big Business to take direct control of the government apparatus. The victory of the Republican Party opened a new stage in the political development of the United States. Breaking the 20-year coalition between the labor bureaucracy and the capitalist state cultivated under Roosevelt and Truman, it ended the equilibrium that had been achieved. All the reactionary, anti-labor tendencies in the country were enormously accelerated.

The coalition, the aim of which was to tie the labor bureaucrats—and through them the trade unions—to the state, was different from similar coalitions in Europe. The workers had no mass political organization of their own, and the labor bureaucrats were granted no government posts. This peculiar feature of the American version of coalitionism (or "Peoples Frontism") underlined the contradiction between the enormous potential strength of the unions and the feeble political weight of the labor bureaucracy in the structure of capitalist politics. The very weakness of the labor bureaucracy made more certain their docility as junior partners and tied them all the tighter to the state, occasional protests notwithstanding.

The political neutralization of the American working class by this process permitted the swing toward capitalist reaction to gain extraordinary momentum and weight. The point was quickly reached where the "coalition" itself could be dispensed with. And in turn the end of the coalition further accelerated the speed and depth of capitalist reaction.

The end of the coalition did not halt the efforts of Big Business to integrate the unions into the state apparatus. It simply changed the form. Whereas under Roosevelt and Truman it proceeded by and large through agreement and acquiescence of the union heads, under Eisenhower the tendency has been to utilize repressive anti-labor legislation and intimidation of the union bureaucrats. This meant fresh acceleration of all the reactionary, anti-labor tendencies in the country.

New impetus was given the witch hunt; and, in moving toward a new equilibrium of class forces, the most favorable conditions were established for the growth of a fascist wing within the Republican Party.

As a product of the witch hunt, McCarthyism continues to set the pace for the hysteria, but it is more than a witch-hunting excrescence of the capitalist state apparatus. It is a native American fascist movement in the early stages of formation. Having stepped out on the political arena as the murderous foe of the working class, it will not be subdued or contained by the old capitalist parties, even though they take fright, or by the well-meaning liberals or by any other force except the working class itself.

The mass base of McCarthyism is found principally in the middle class but also extends into sections of misguided, backward workers, many of them not organized in unions, segments of the extreme right-wing elements in mass production plants, declassed elements and bourgeois-minded student youth.

The McCarthyites have attracted a fringe of intellectual "theorists" and apologists. This is indicative of the depth of the crisis in the petty-bourgeois intellectual circles. From among the renegades of Marxism as well as from the ranks of the young bourgeois intellectuals, a cadre of fascist publicists and brain trusters is being selected.

The framework of a national fascist organization has already formed around McCarthy. All the fascist groups that flourished in previous periods but could never find a major national leader or focal point have rallied to McCarthy's banner. The Gerald L.K. Smith movement, the Coughlinites, the Christian Fronters, the Ku Klux Klan, the Minute Women, sections of the veterans organizations, vigilante groups, herds of professional scabs, sections of the underworld and the like are now linked by common devotion to the would-be American Hitler, Senator Joseph McCarthy.

The evidence is considerable that McCarthy has wide support among the police, particularly in the larger cities. And of course the sheriffs and deputies of the lynch-ridden South and South West are natural allies of the rising McCarthyite movement.

In the legislative branch of the government, McCarthy has about 15 Senators, including Jenner, Mundt, Dirksen, and Butler. These are not necessarily fascist politicians. Some are merely reactionaries playing McCarthy's game for the moment. But they help further the fascist movement and constitute a strong segment of the apparatus at McCarthy's command.

In the executive department, McCarthy's influence is extensive. The Army-McCarthy hearings revealed to what lengths the professional military caste are prepared to go in conciliating the fascist Senator and cooperating with his aims. Even more illuminating is the growing encroachment of McCarthy's lieutenant Scott McLeod in the State Department. This fascist has set up a super-secret police apparatus that acts as a rival administrative command to Dulles himself.

On the financial side, McCarthy is supported by a group of fabulously wealthy oil tycoons of Texas. This is one of the most ominous signs of the growing power of the fascist movement. This section of the capitalist class not only supplies vast monetary resources, it constitutes a point of contact with other capitalists who can be recruited as backers of McCarthy. While they are a relatively new sector of Big Business and far from the decisive power in the capitalist class, their power is growing and they constitute the initial recruits for fascism in America's ruling class.

All attempts of the Democrats and Republicans to curb, crush, outflank, or brush aside McCarthy have ended in fiasco. The Army-McCarthy hearings, for instance, which resulted from the need of the Eisenhower administration to draw a line on the encroachments of McCarthy's independent power, cost nothing more to the fascist demagogue than the sacrifice of his Jewish Democratic attorney as a scapegoat.

On the other hand, the hearings counted as combat experience for McCarthy's mass following. All evidence shows that the basic core became hardened and drew more closely around the banner of the fascist demagogue. It is true that some marginal supporters were repelled by the crudity of McCarthy's conduct. But the idea that this constituted a major setback for the fascist movement is nothing short of insane. The rise of Hitler likewise had its passionate division of the middle class for and against, with innumerable shifts and upsets. As a matter of fact, the very posing in the hearings of the question "for or against McCarthy?" constituted a major advance for American fascism. Moreover, the hearings brought into focus for millions the indispensable personal symbolism of the leader in the national political arena. There it will stay until the working class settles the issue definitively.

The struggle that broke into the open at the Army-McCarthy hearings showed most clearly that McCarthy's movement is not just another political clique that can be disposed of by the capitalist machine politicians once it transcends the limits of what is permissible in the code of bourgeois democratic politics. It is a new type of machine with independent power resting on a mass base of its own.

The hearings revealed both the depth of the cleavage between the two wings of the capitalist witch hunters and the inability of the Eisenhower Republican and Democratic opponents of McCarthy to really smash the fascist's power. The basic reason for this impotence is that while an intolerable antagonism exists between the bourgeois state in its democratic form (even though it has been considerably modified in the direction of reaction) and the fascist form, nevertheless in the period of the death agony of capitalism, the bourgeois democratic government itself prepares the ground, sows the seed, cultivates and nourishes the development of fascism. The working class alone can cut this development short and save America from the catastrophe of a fascist dictatorship. But for this the workers must take power and extend democracy into the heart of industry on the basis of the socialist reconstruction of American society.

McCarthy's role as the architect of an American fascist movement is perhaps nowhere more vividly manifested than in his use of the blackmail technique. Blackmail is a favorite weapon of fascist demagogues. McCarthy, who has studied *Mein Kampf* very carefully, has taken a cue from Hitler, who was also able to make powerful use of the corruption that flourishes among democratic capitalist politicians in order to make them play the Nazi game in critical situations.

Like Hitler's charge of "14 years of shame and treason," McCarthy's charge of "20 or 21 years of treason," which he levels against the Democrats and somewhat more carefully but nevertheless plainly against Eisenhower, is the pivot of fascist demagogy. The treason charge marks the boundary between the official witch hunt and its unofficial fascist offspring. In a sense it constitutes the witch hunting of the witch hunters. While the official witch hunters boast about having crushed the domestic "communist menace," although continuing to whip up the hysteria over an alleged communist menace abroad, the McCarthyites charge that the U.S. government has been infested with conscious and unconscious Russian agents for two decades and more. They claim that the highest military circles deliberately handed half of Germany and all of China to Moscow. They claim that the government is still honey-combed with spies and traitors.

The treason charge provides the peg for two further points that are crucial to the development of fascism. First, it is the basis for full fledged social demagogy as the crisis deepens. It already appeals to the disoriented and disturbed layers of the middle class, since all their woes, anxieties, fears, economic troubles, can be blamed on treasonous conspirators who sold America out to the Russians. It gives McCarthy the basis to parade before the people as their tribune and the avenger of the wrongs done them.

Second, the treason charge offers a convenient formula for taking power. As the fascists gain in strength they can step up the hysteria over this accusation. Use of the treason formula along this line was already apparent in the Army-McCarthy hearings. McCarthy called on the officers and government functionaries to funnel confidential information to him on anything involving "security." As the outraged McCarthy opponents pointed out, he asked these officials and civil service employees to violate their oath of office. McCarthy's reply was simple. The oath of office can be observed in essence only by violating its form because of the treasonous conduct of government heads due to laxity, stupidity ... or worse. This appeal for recruits was undoubtedly effective among careerists and those with fascist inclinations.

The unity of the developing fascist movement and the official witch hunters is revealed basically in their common defense and advocacy of capitalism. More immediately their unity is revealed in common agreement on the witch-hunting formula: that is, that a "communist menace" exists and that it must be cut out root and branch. Their difference is expressed in disagreement over how this is to be achieved. The official witch hunters give lip service to democratic and parliamentary forms; the fascists advocate rougher methods. Thus a rivalry exists in the witch-hunting field between the Eisenhower-Truman wing and the McCarthyites. Since the McCarthy wing does not hold power, while police-state legislation has been actually passed, first under Truman then under Eisenhower, it may seem that the greatest danger to democratic rights and civil liberties comes from the old-line political machines. This conclusion, however, is a mistake.

In the rivalry for preeminence in the witch-hunting field, the fascist tendency is the final winner. Truman's witch hunting, for example, turned out to be simply preparation for the ascendancy of Brownellism which did not hesitate to turn the witch-hunting guns on Truman himself. Brownellism likewise simply prepares for the ascendancy of McCarthy. All the witch hunting of the Eisenhower regime has not saved Eisenhower himself from becoming McCarthy's target. In fact Eisenhower's witch hunting constituted essential preparation for his own victimization.

The mechanics of this process is quite simple. Having conceded McCarthy's basic formula of the "communist menace," the official witch hunters are caught in a dilemma. If they do not step up the witch hunt, if they fail to continue to load the statutes with police-state measures, they are obviously being "soft on communism." McCarthy is the gainer. On the other hand, if they become more rabid and enact new savagely antidemocratic laws, they confirm McCarthy's basic formula and thereby enhance his prestige. To attack him then gives him the aura of a martyr. Doing McCarthy's work does not weaken him, it strengthens his entire position. The history of Hitler's rise in Germany is especially rich in lessons in this ABC of politics.

To think that Brownellism is a graver menace than McCarthyism is to grossly underestimate what would happen in America with McCarthy in the White House. This does not mean that Brownellism must be taken as a "lesser evil" than McCarthyism; the whole point is that McCarthyism must be fought by undertaking to oust both Republicans and Democrats from office and replacing them by a Workers and Farmers Government.

The cleavage between what has been most recently called "Brownellism," after Eisenhower's attorney general, and McCarthyism, is a cleavage between the Bonapartist and fascist tendencies that have appeared on the American political scene. Just as we characterize McCarthyism as incipient fascism, so we must designate the drift toward police statism in the ruling structure of American capitalism as budding Bonapartism.

In his analysis of the political situation in Germany immediately before Hitler took power, Trotsky characterized Bonapartism, or the "caricature of Bonapartism," as "a regime of military-police dictatorship." He defined the conditions for the rise of Bonapartism in the epoch of capitalist decline as follows:

"As soon as the struggle of the two social strata—the haves and the have-nots, the exploiter and the exploited—reaches its highest tension, the conditions are given for the domination of bureaucracy, police, soldiery . . . To be sure, such a government does not cease being a clerk of the property owners." (The Only Road)

Trotsky distinguished between the Bonapartism of the immediate pre-fascist period and a relatively stable Bonapartism of capitalist rule as follows:

"The Bonapartist regime can attain a comparatively stable and durable character only in the event that it brings a revolutionary epoch to a close; when the relationship of forces has already been tested in battles; when the revolutionary classes are already spent; while the possessing classes have not yet freed themselves from the fear: will not the morrow bring new convulsions? Without this basic condition, that is, without a preceding exhaustion of mass energies in battles, the Bonapartist regime is in no position to develop."

Elements of Bonapartism in the capitalist government have been growing in the United States since the emergence of the American working class as a colossal power in the Thirties. With the appearance of industrial unions, the United States became a house divided. Every major pulsation of the working-class struggle has tended to pose the question of who will be master. Every struggle, no matter how restricted its initial form, has tended to become a showdown struggle between the two powerful antagonists, American capitalism and the working class.

Under these conditions Bonapartist tendencies became quite marked. Roosevelt's infamous formula: "A plague on both your houses" during the Little Steel strike of 1937 when the workers were hit by a strike-breaking assault (Mohawk Valley Formula) was an expression of precisely this tendency.

During the Roosevelt and Truman administrations, the tendency toward Bonapartism—in particular American forms—can be traced in the feverish growth of the central state apparatus, the increased power of the military brass, the emergence of the secret political police (FBI) as a major independent entity within the government, the increase of the President's "emergency" powers (even to commit the country to war as in the Korean "police action"), and finally in the officially sponsored nationwide witch hunt.

The partiality of the American capitalists for "Brownellism" at present, and their current hostility toward the "path of McCarthy" is shown by their yearning for an "economical road to fascism," or, as Trotsky characterized the Bonapartist policy of the French bourgeoisie in the pre-World War II period, "fascism on the cheap."

In our definitions of both McCarthyism and Bonapartism, where we draw heavily on the European experience, it is necessary to guard due proportions. What we have is an anticipatory mobilization of the political forces threatening to atomize the American proletariat. These forces show a marked maturity even before the full consequences of the social crisis have appeared in the United States. The maturity of the tendency toward a "preventive" reactionary settlement with the working class stems, as we have indicated, from the desperate position of American capitalism in the world arena on the one hand, and on the other from the labor bureaucracy's strangulation of the independent class movement of the workers.

## Perspective of American fascism

We say that American fascism is "incipient." By that we do not intend to minimize the danger. The fascist movement always remains incipient until a major default by the working class in one or more revolutionary situations permits the fascist movement to develop into a more advanced form. This occurs when successive defaults alienate the middle class to such an extent that the fascist demagogue can mobilize the ruined and crazed section into effective shock brigades for a counter-revolutionary civil war against the working class.

McCarthyism has not reached that stage and there is every reason to believe that the American working class can be mobilized to crush it before it ever reaches that stage. But there are a number of features about American fascism that are different from its European forerunners. That such a formidable mobilization of the fascists has already taken place before the social crisis of American capitalism has led to the mass radicalization of the working class as a polarizing center for the middle class, is a fact that must be assessed and understood.

The powerful initial flush of American fascism stems from the weakened world position of the United States. The reflex of the ruling class, transmitted through a witch hunt of unprecedented scope, intensity and duration, has served to channelize the deep disturbances in the middle class in the direction of McCarthyism. This is one of the consequences of a default in leadership by the American working class due to the paralyzing role of the labor bureaucracy. After the rise of the CIO the bureaucrats managed to block formation of an independent Labor Party that would have attracted the middle classes. During World War II, they supported Roosevelt and his war policy, once more refusing to take the road that could have attracted a middle class that was uneasy over the slaughter and its consequences. Finally, in the Korean experience, the labor bureaucrats again supported Truman and the war-mongers in the teeth of mass opposition to the adventure, not only among the workers but among the middle class, primarily the farmers. These successive defaults of leadership made possible the present turn toward McCarthyism by considerable sections of the middle class who find no other means, in the absence of working-class leadership, of expressing their discontent and nervousness.

Thus taking the political scene as a whole, the mass character of McCarthy's following in a certain sense constitutes an anticipatory counter-formation to the coming radicalization of the working class, a radicalization that can be expected to take explosive forms.

With a sharp upsurge of radicalism among the workers this initial advantage enjoyed by American fascism can be rapidly reversed. The McCarthyites would become isolated. The greatest danger then would be the wave of illusion, assiduously nurtured by the Stalinists and the labor bureaucrats, that fascism had been defeated and that a new coalition with the liberal capitalists would bar its resurgence.

What about a different variant; namely, a "cold" victory for the fascists? If McCarthy, for instance, captures control of the Republican Party and becomes its presidential candidate, say in 1956, would this open the possibility for a fascist regime to come to power? Would this mean that the working class had been denied its historic opportunity to establish a Workers and Farmers Government?

It is not excluded that McCarthy and those around him can be absorbed by the Republican machine. If they do so merely as individuals then we would have witnessed the dissolution of a group of leaders of incipient fascism into the basic bourgeois democratic political machine which has more and more tended to set up a Bonapartist police state regime characterized by the enormous power of the military and of the secret political police. This type of withdrawal was seen in the case of Mayor Hague, a potential candidate for the role of American Hitler in the late thirties. But if McCarthy follows this course, the role of fascist leader will fall to someone else who will pick up the strings by denouncing McCarthy's "treason and betrayal."

Another possibility is that McCarthy in the White House utilizes this position to mobilize the middle class against the workers and their organizations. This would give him maximum "legal" cover for an all-out fight to consolidate his power and carry out his fascist program. For the working class it would mean a desperate struggle to safeguard the Bill of Rights from subversion by the highest official in the land. The historic opportunity of the working class to put a Workers and Farmers Government in power would then occur in a different form and under more difficult circumstances than if they had mobilized earlier.

At present, however, the tendency of development is along different lines marked by the growing cleavage between the Bonapartist wing and the fascist wing.

A temporary deal with the Soviet Union would deepen this cleavage, as the economic and social crisis in America grew more profound. The outbreak of war, on the other hand, would give the Bonapartist elements, Eisenhower-Brownell, etc., the upper hand and enormously strengthen the trend toward a police state. The distinctive fascist tendencies might even be smothered by such a turn of events. At the next stage, when the hopeless war brought ruin and devastation and frightful suffering, the polarization of the country into a fascist and a revolutionary proletarian camp would proceed with terrific speed.

# 4. MCCARTHY—A 'BOURGEOIS DEMOCRAT'? A REPLY TO VERN AND RYAN

By Joseph Hansen

The following article, reprinted from SWP *Discussion Bulletin* A-25 in 1954, was written in reply to the "Resolution on McCarthyism" by Dennis Vern and Sam Ryan, which appears in SWP *Discussion Bulletin* A-24 in 1954. Vern and Ryan were the leaders of a small tendency in the Los Angeles local of the SWP which took shape during the discussion of the nature of the Eastern European states in the early 1950s. Vern and Ryan claimed that these states became workers' states as soon as they were occupied by the Soviet army, resting their case on a garbled version of Lenin's *State and Revolution.* Their differences eventually spread to all areas of political life and, at the end of 1954, they walked out of the party to join Shachtman's Independent Socialist League.

In their "Resolution on 'McCarthyism,'" (SWP *Discussion Bulletin* A-24, November 1954) Dennis Vern and Sam Ryan take the curious position that McCarthy is only a "bourgeois democrat." As a counter-weight to this they take the still more curious position that all bourgeois democrats are "potential fascists." From this they draw the conclusion that a campaign that singles out McCarthyism as the American form of fascism is ill-advised and even helps prop up the bourgeois order. "The net effect of this campaign is not to hurt McCarthy, or the bourgeois state, but to excuse the bourgeois state for the indisputable evidences of its bourgeois character, and thus hinder the proletariat in its understanding that the bourgeois-democratic state is an 'executive committee' of the capitalist class, and that only *a workers state* can offer an appropriate objective for the class struggle." (Emphasis by Vern-Ryan, as in all cases where I quote them.)

To make a complete analysis of the Vern-Ryan position, to untangle everything they tangle up, and put in proper perspective the things they do have right would keep the mimeograph tied up for quite a while; and the analysis, I am afraid, would tend to become as boring and tough to chew on as its subject matter. I propose therefore only to take up the most glaring faults of the Vern-Ryan resolution and let it go at that.

The fundamental error in the Vern-Ryan position on McCarthyism, apparent in the first paragraph of their document, is methodological: ". . . a wide range of American politicians, from Senators Humphrey and Douglas on one hand, to McCarran and Dirksen, on the other, are all *potential* fascists. . . ." This "fascist potentiality," derives from their "support of the capitalist order." And the capitalist order infuses them with fascist potentiality because "in certain circumstances capitalism can be temporarily maintained only through the intercession of fascism."

This position is carried with dispatch to its logical absurdity in the second paragraph of the document: "Any supporter of the capitalist system, is by virtue of that support, *a potential fascist.* . . ."

How shall we apply that theory? Shall we say, for instance, that the Social Democrats, having betrayed Marxism, objectively support the capitalist order; and that therefore, all Social Democrats are potential fascists? And since every beast must have its name, shall we call the Social Democrats—social fascists?

Vern and Ryan, we hope, will note the close resemblance of that position to the one with which the Stalinists helped pave the way for Hitler.

Naturally they will object, and with justice, that they drew precisely the opposite conclusion from their premises—that none of the capitalist politicians in Washington are actual fascists, not even McCarthy; they are all "bourgeois democrats." I will readily grant that this conclusion is inescapable from the premises on which Vern and Ryan stand. I only call attention to the fact that precisely the opposite conclusion is equally inescapable—they are all fascists.

We are caught in this mire because of the impulsion Vern and Ryan feel to make McCarthy out as anything but a fascist. If he is not a fascist, he must be a bourgeois democrat. If this is true of McCarthy, it must be all the more true of the other current capitalist politicians. Where then will the fascist politicians eventually come from? Either something totally new and unexpected will appear or the bourgeois democrats will become fascists. But if they can turn into fascists, it becomes of crucial importance to determine the point of qualitative change.

Out of this mire, by spontaneous generation as in the days when formal logic ruled supreme, arise the categories Vern and Ryan need—"potential fascist" now-a-bourgeois-democrat, "actual fascist" was-a-bourgeois-democrat, and the "two inescapable and basically essential features," which we will consider later, that determine when a bourgeois democrat becomes a fascist.

As we have seen already, however, it doesn't require a very powerful lens to discover that a potential fascist is an actual fascist and that therefore all of Vern-Ryan's "bourgeois democrats" are fascists. Something, it would appear, is wrong with premises that permit such latitude in the conclusion to be drawn from them. What is it?

Let us examine the links of the chain of reasoning offered us by Vern and Ryan: (1) At a certain stage the capitalist order can be maintained only through fascism. (2) Anyone who supports the capitalist order must therefore eventually accept fascism. (3) Anyone who eventually accepts fascism is a potential fascist. (4) Since all capitalist politicians support the capitalist order, they are all potential fascists.

The error in logic is a gross one. It is known technically as the Fallacy of Division. What is true of something as a whole is mistakenly held to be equally true of each of its parts. For example: "Common table salt, a compound of chlorine and sodium, is good on french-fried potatoes. Therefore, chlorine and sodium is good on french-fried potatoes." But chlorine is a poisonous gas and sodium a light metal that would react most violently when it touched one's mouth, if it hadn't done so already on the potatoes.

The fact that Vern and Ryan were probably ignorant of the name of their error is no excuse for having committed it. It is possible to think straight without being a trained logician, although I will readily grant that a little training helps. In the case of Vern and Ryan it might have helped them avoid becoming so dazzled by words like "potential" and "actual." Both Vern and Ryan are perfectly aware that the capitalist order as a whole evolves toward a fascist stage and is therefore not only "potentially" fascist but "actually" fascist in tendency. An ounce of thought should have shown that this premise does not permit us to conclude that *all* capitalist politicians are "potential" fascists or "actual" fascists in tendency even though they all support the capitalist order. Historically the capitalist class as a whole supports fascism, but not all its parts. And the "whole" can be represented by the economically dominant minority.

Had Vern and Ryan used the dialectic method, they would have been less likely to commit such a blunder. They saw what was common in fascists and liberals—both species of politicians support the capitalist order. It was an achievement to see this and a good illustration of the fact that formal logic, even unconscious formal logic, has a certain power. The dialectician, however, begins with that. Having discovered the "one"—what unites the fascist and liberal politicians—he turns his attention to "division of the one"; that is, the difference between them. It doesn't require much analysis to indicate that the difference can develop into contradiction. Historical experience shows us that heads can roll, particularly the heads of liberals—even though they faithfully support the capitalist order. In fact, it is precisely because they faithfully support the capitalist order that their heads roll.

This paradox would remain inexplicable if we stayed at the level that sees only the unity between fascists and liberals. To the logic of contradiction, however, the paradox is easily resolvable. First of all, capitalist politicians are interested primarily in the welfare of a particular section of the class they represent. Differences in particular interests can lead to sharp clashes between capitalist politicians, as we see every day, not only between major machines but within the machines. A capitalist politician tends to become identified with the interests of a particular group and the changes in the relative weight and importance of the group are projected on the national political scene as changes in his personal standing. Since the development of capitalism itself pushes to the forefront successive economic groupings, these are reflected in a succession of different types of politicians. In this framework, personal characteristics play a considerable role in the choice of individuals to play these leading roles. We may be sure, for instance, that Taft's innermost convictions were a faithful reflection of the outlook of the Cleveland real-estate barons and that he acted in full sincerity out of those convictions. That was an essential personal requirement to achieve leadership of the grouping. At that stage of capitalist development where the general interests of the system are best expressed in democratic forms of rule, the particular grouping whose interests most closely coincide with those forms will be found dominant and its individual politicians take the center of the stage. When the general interests of the system come into contradiction with democratic forms, this signifies that a different grouping has come to the forefront, and along with it, with more or less delay, a different set of political leaders.

I have stated this in the most condensed and abstract way with the understanding that in actual life these generalities are subject to considerable modification. However, we must begin with such abstractions to find the points of departure for our own policies in the national arena.

For instance, if a regime that rules in principle through democratic forms is threatened by the rise of a fascist movement (which is committed in principle to the destruction of democratic forms), it would be a fatal error to consider the liberal regime as potentially fascist. And it would be just as fatal not to recognize the real character of the fascist movement and to consider it only "bourgeois democratic." In fact the two errors are simply two sides of a single fault—*incapacity to differentiate.* The truth is, that as the capitalist representatives of democratic forms, the liberals are threatened with annihilation at the hands of the fascists. But democratic forms include freedom of speech, of assembly, of the press and the right to organize in unions and political parties. In a struggle involving those rights, the working class cannot stand aside. To do so would mean its own atomization at the hands of the fascists.

Let us look once again at the opening paragraph of the Vern-Ryan document: ". . . a wide range of American politicians, from Senator Humphrey and Douglas on one hand, to McCarran and Dirksen, on the other, are all *potential* fascists. . . ." Giving the authors of that concept the benefit of the doubt, perhaps we should assume that, confused over the complex inter-relationship between liberals like Humphrey and Douglas and fascists like McCarthy, they impatiently decided to dispose of the problem by considering them all one reactionary mass and labelling them inappropriately enough— "bourgeois democrats." The proposed solution, it must be admitted, has the attraction of simplicity if nothing else.

Liberals like Humphrey and Douglas feel threatened by fascists like McCarthy. They also feel insecure, quailing at what must seem to them virtually impossible tasks—maintaining prosperity and carrying forward the war program to its conclusion. They have lost confidence in the efficacy of democratic forms, which means that as politicians they have lost confidence in themselves and their own future. Nevertheless, they cling desperately to their positions and attempt to shore them up. Thus in face of the pressure from McCarthy, they even try to go him one better. They try to outflank the fascist. Hence their prominence in espousing such legislation as outlawing the Communist Party. Superficially they thus appear even worse than McCarthy. From their viewpoint, however, it is only protective coloration. They still remain liberals. And they are right; they are only liberals. All their witch hunting will not save them should McCarthyism come to power.

Fascists like McCarthy, on the other hand, feel in tune with the times. Despite the blows and setbacks they take as well as give, they display confidence in themselves and their future as if they knew that so far as the capitalist system is concerned, their turn is next, even though it may take a few years. Hence their arrogance and their contempt for the liberals of both parties. They can afford to let the liberals run interference on witch-hunt legislation; it helps them, just as the witch hunt itself prepared the way for their entry as major figures on the political arena although the witch hunt was not started by them but by the Democrats under Truman. Ironically, the very measures the liberals sponsor in their own search for protective coloration provide protective coloration for the McCarthyites in extending the witch hunt and building their own forces. It's all been legalized with the blessings of the liberals.

In this contest between the liberals and the fascists should the working class abstain with a curse on both their houses? Should we follow the method of Vern and Ryan and refuse to separate McCarthy "in any way from all the other supporters of capitalism" and call him, as they do, nothing but another "bourgeois democrat"? To do so would be to follow the politics of abstention and actually facilitate McCarthy's work.

The correct course is based on the major differentiation between the liberals and fascists. We defend the democratic forms against the fascist threat. We do so by attacking the liberals for capitulating to the fascists, for performing their own historic function of paving the way for the fascists, for betraying the people to McCarthyism. From the concessions the liberals make to the fascists—concessions of deep injury to the labor movement—we demonstrate the necessity of removing the liberals from power. We fight to replace them with working-class politicians at the head of an independent labor political movement capable of defending labor's rights and gains and of stopping McCarthyism. And to accomplish that task we level our fire in the labor movement at the bureaucrats who support the liberals and thereby stand in the way of truly representing labor's interests and of smashing the fascist threat. Is that so difficult to understand?

## How to tell a fascist from a liberal

To concretize our analysis still further, let us make one more observation about the inter-relationship between liberals and fascists. If McCarthyism should succeed in mobilizing the middle class and getting the nod from Wall Street, it can be expected that some liberal politicians would knock at fascist headquarters for entrance and assignment to posts in the movement, no matter how modest—even posts as window dressing. A few would undoubtedly be accepted. The youngest of them might succeed in living down their "red" past and carving out some kind of career in the fascist machine. The older ones would be nothing but pitiful captives. On the other hand, if the McCarthyites were dealt a major defeat we could expect a share of them to appear hat in hand before the Republican and Democratic machine bosses, and there would be no doubt whatsoever that some of them would be absorbed as part of the effort to liquidate them as an opposition.

At this point, I suppose, we might expect Vern and Ryan to demand a minute to ask a "damaging" question: "First you admit that the so-called liberals try to outdo McCarthy in passing police-state legislation and even succeed in this. Then you admit that liberals can become fascists, which is what we contended all along, and that fascists can also switch over. In view of this, would you mind informing us just how you propose to tell a fascist from a liberal if you reject our position? It seems to us that you have helped confirm what we pointed out in our document; namely, that in determining 'the *lowest* common denominator' you cannot have less than its promulgation of a 'radical' program and organization of 'special bodies of armed men.' To quote from our document: 'These two features—a radical program of 'anti-capitalism' and special armed gangs—furnish the two inescapable and basically essential features of a fascist movement.' Consequently, so far as McCarthyism is concerned, 'Until the movement outlines a 'radical' program and organizes special bodies of armed men around it, it may be a reactionary and a dangerous movement, *but it is not fascist,* and will very likely degenerate into the well stocked limbo of previous middle class movements.'"

The fact that Vern and Ryan are prepared to recognize that McCarthyism can be termed "fascist" if and when it advances a "radical" program and "organizes special bodies of armed men around it" is to be welcomed. At that time we may look forward to finding ourselves in common agreement in our analysis of the movement and what should be done about it. Meanwhile, however, we face a political problem that cannot be evaded: What should be done right now to prepare the working class so that it can properly defend itself if and when McCarthyism advances a "radical" program and "organizes special bodies of armed men around it"? Or can we complacently adopt the Vern-Ryan position and assure the working class that McCarthyism "will very likely degenerate into the well stocked limbo of previous middle class movements"? The posing of the problem shows at once how sharply the Vern-Ryan position diverges from the program of action needed to really cause McCarthyism to "degenerate."

Is our science so limited that we cannot tell a fascist movement until its "two inescapable and basically essential features" have reached full-blown forms? Are we forced to call its leaders "bourgeois democrats" before then? It seems to me that we should be able to do better than that. Let us start with ordinary common sense.

As Vern and Ryan observe, "Senator McCarthy has been branded a fascist over a number of years now by a great many bourgeois politicians such as Tydings, Flanders, Benton, Eisenhower's brother, Mrs. Roosevelt, and Adlai Stevenson." To this evidence, our spetzes respond, "Marxism disagrees." The common opinion of the bourgeois politicians is brushed aside because McCarthyism doesn't fit in with the preconceived ideas of Vern and Ryan. Naturally we must disregard factional exaggerations made by the bourgeois opponents of McCarthy but also we must note the damage that is done them by their admission. What do they have to gain as supporters of capitalism by confessing that American capitalism has spawned—a fascist movement? In addition, we should note this important fact, which seems to have escaped Vern and Ryan, that these bourgeois politicians represent leading figures in both the Republican and Democratic parties. They do not consider McCarthy a specifically *Republican* phenomenon, but something apart and in opposition to *both* parties. The unanimity of opinion, furthermore, shows that it does not represent individual aberrations, but represents the general view in America's ruling circles. Those circles should know what McCarthy is.

In this respect, one outstanding fact alone must be duly weighed; that is the financial support a section of the ruling class is already providing McCarthy. Do Vern and Ryan actually believe that the Texas oil tycoons consider McCarthy only another—bourgeois democrat? Or lacking the advantages of Marxist method, have the Texas billionaires made a mistake, feeding oats to the wrong horse?

If it is any consolation to Vern and Ryan, it can be expected that these ruling circles and the bourgeois politicians, who now admit that McCarthy is a fascist, may in the future adopt the Vern-Ryan position—that McCarthy is only another "bourgeois democrat." That will be about the time they decide to turn to the fascist solution; and McCarthy, advancing his "radical" program and organizing "special bodies of armed men," needs such propagandistic camouflage. What will Vern and Ryan then say about the earlier admissions of the bourgeois politicians?

In addition to the evidence from bourgeois ruling circles that McCarthy is a fascist, we have the evidence of European opinion. Vern and Ryan leave this completely out of consideration, yet it is based on the most solid grounds—actual experience in the rise of a number of fascist movements that have displayed considerable differences. Are we to simply dismiss the warning of European public opinion, which is virtually unanimous in considering McCarthy a fascist and which has been shouting to the American people to wake up, heed what happened in Italy, Germany, and Spain, and take action while McCarthyism is still weak? To brush aside that opinion, as Vern and Ryan do, is to close our ears to the voice of experience in order to avoid profaning the preconceived forms we demand that McCarthyism meet before we will grudgingly concede that it is indeed a fascist movement. The experience of the European working class, earned at such cost, deserves better from us.

Still confining ourselves to the empiric level, let us take another look at McCarthy himself. Here, I offer in evidence the opinions of Vern and Ryan, stripped however of their theoretical interpretation. We have already seen that the Vern-Ryan use of the "potential-actual" categories constituted a gross error in logic. Through the error they were able to take the actual fascist McCarthy, convert him into a "potential" fascist, and therefore through their wrong method into nothing but a "bourgeois democrat." By pointing out the error, we topple the entire Vern-Ryan construction with one kick. But out of the ruin we are able to salvage a few bricks. For instance, they admit that McCarthy "does have personal qualities that equip him for fascism's task." How did they arrive at that conclusion? By what criteria? Obviously in the same way that such people as Flanders, Eisenhower's brother, Mrs. Roosevelt, and Adlai Stevenson did. Through observing McCarthy in action.

They go even further. "McCarthy has openly been—(possibly as part of a conscious plan to present himself some day as an American fascist leader)—not even as 'anti-labor' as some of the other bourgeois democrats." How did Vern and Ryan reach the conclusion that McCarthy may be operating today with a "conscious plan" to present himself in the future as "an American fascist leader"? By what criteria? Again, obviously, by observing McCarthy in action. But isn't a politician who follows a conscious plan to present himself as a fascist leader an *actual* fascist? Most telling of all is the recognition by Vern and Ryan of McCarthy's obvious purpose—to appear "not even as 'anti-labor' as some of the other bourgeois democrats." Doesn't that very fact give an intimation of McCarthy's *potential* capacity to use radical-sounding demagogy?

So far we have confined ourselves to only some of the facts that hit you in the eye. Let us extend our range a bit and see what we can turn up. In accordance with the Marxist method, we must examine the origin of McCarthyism, something Vern and Ryan forgot to do. The record is absolutely clear. When McCarthy first won national prominence in 1950, we noted that he had done so through a "super witch hunt." This was an obvious fact, but our conclusion is also interesting from the viewpoint of methodology. As Marxists we noted a qualitative difference in the witch hunt. We "differentiated," found "a division of the one." Then we followed the development of that difference until it became so great that the author of the witch hunt, Truman, was himself witch-hunted. We were cautious, even conservative about applying our label. However, when not only Truman, but at the same time, Eisenhower in the White House, was witch-hunted; when it was clear that McCarthy had a large middle-class backing, that he was organizing independently, that every fascist grouping known to us since 1937 was hailing him as leader, no mistake was possible—a fascist movement had crystallized out of the witch hunt. That was when we put the correct label on McCarthyism as the American form of fascism. The fear, and even panic, of such well-known liberals as Humphrey, Douglas, Lehman, and the rest, in face of McCarthy's rise only confirmed the correctness of the designation.

In contrast to this method of determining the difference between McCarthyism and the bourgeois democracy that spawned it, note the position of Vern and Ryan: "Fascism in America will not arrive as an integral part of the present witch hunt; it is ironic but true that *it is not the success but the failure* of the witch hunt that will force American capitalism to take the fascist path."

McCarthyism is an "integral part of the present witch hunt." That's absolutely true. And it's just as absolutely not true. Vern and Ryan do not see any differentiation in the witch hunt. They view it statically. The witch hunt is only a witch hunt. "A"="A." And "A" can't possibly equal anything else. Small wonder they are unable to see a fascist movement proceeding from the witch hunt. But viewing it dynamically and not statically, that is, dialectically and not purely formally, can we say that the witch hunt is still what it was when Truman started it? Did Truman begin by witch-hunting himself? Did McCarthy set the pace in 1947? By what magic did McCarthy come to national prominence if there was no internal differentiation in the witch hunt?

The static, pigeon-hole approach leads Vern and Ryan into a further serious deviation from Marxist method. The witch hunt, if I interpret them correctly, is a single chapter that will fail, leaving us with nothing new as a heritage of its existence. It will drop into the "limbo" as one of a series that have dropped into that chute like empty tomato cans. Something else, perhaps unforeseen will then develop. Maybe even a movement headed by such bourgeois democrats as Douglas or Humphrey or Lehman! Who knows? This will finally prove to be genuine fascism. The intermediate links are thus left out completely. Vern and Ryan have failed to take into consideration the continuity of American fascism.

Although in obverse form, this is in essence the same methodological error committed by the Cochranites in relation to the continuity of the revolutionary socialist movement in America. The Cochranites crossed off the past of the revolutionary movement and, for the future, think something novel, without any links with the past, will emerge. Vern and Ryan utilize the same method in relation to fascism in the U.S.

They do not grasp the central fact that so far as the development of capitalist politics is concerned, the "success" of the witch hunt is manifest precisely in the emergence of McCarthyism; that is, the American form of fascism. To conclude that the witch hunt has succeeded only in grouping the "lunatic right wing fringe" behind McCarthy, to use the words of Vern and Ryan, is to repeat the error of those who considered Hitler nothing but a "lunatic" at the head of a "lunatic right wing fringe." What is most lunatic is to repeat such an error with McCarthy after the experience with Hitler. It is an instructive example, however, of how similar methods lead to similar results.

**Vern and Ryan set Trotsky straight**

The reference in the draft resolution to Mayor Hague of Jersey City is picked up by Vern and Ryan for a dissertation on what they consider to be an error by Trotsky. The pertinent quotations are taken from a transcript of a discussion with Trotsky published in the Feb. 1946 *Fourth International*. The entire discussion deserves careful study, but here we will confine ourselves to the alleged error.

"In the United States it might be different but the fundamental tasks are the same," Trotsky said. "I read about the tactics of Hague. It is a rehearsal of a Fascist overthrow. He represents small bosses who became infuriated because the crisis deepened. He has his gang which is absolutely unconstitutional. This is very, very contagious. With the deepening of the crisis it will spread all over the country and Roosevelt who is a very good democrat will say, 'Perhaps it is the only solution.'

"It was the same in Italy. They had a minister who invited the Socialists. The Socialists refused. He admitted the Fascists. He thought he could balance them against the Socialists, but they smashed the minister too. Now I think the example of New Jersey is very important. We should utilize everything, but this especially."

Further on, Trotsky continues: "In Newark the Mayor begins to imitate Hague and they are all inspired by Hague and by the big bosses. It is absolutely certain that Roosevelt will observe that now in the crisis he can do nothing with democratic means. He is not a fascist as the Stalinists claimed in 1932. (Or a "potential" fascist—J.H.) But his initiative will be paralyzed. What can he do? The workers are dissatisfied. The big bosses are dissatisfied. He can only maneuver until the end of his term and then say goodbye. A third term for Roosevelt is absolutely excluded.

"The imitation of the Newark mayor has tremendous importance. In two or three years you can have a powerful fascist movement of American character. What is Hague? He has nothing to do with Mussolini or Hitler, but he is an American fascist. Why is he aroused? Because the society can no longer be run by democratic means.

"It would of course be impermissible to fall into hysteria. The danger of the working class being out-run by events is indisputable, but we can combat this danger only by energetic, systematic development of our own activity and under adequate revolutionary slogans and not by fantastic efforts to spring over our own heads."

Now let's hear from Vern and Ryan. "It would be futile, and the evidence of a conception of Trotsky as some kind of infallible 'Pope,' were one to deny that this analysis is primarily incorrect. A third and a fourth term for Roosevelt was clearly not 'absolutely excluded'; Roosevelt did not observe that in the crisis he can do nothing 'with democratic means'; nor was his initiative 'paralyzed'; he did not maneuver until the end of his term 'and then say goodbye' (except in Sinclair Lewis' book). With his accustomed bourgeois democratic methods Roosevelt maintained the democratic state as an adequate instrument of the American capitalist class, was elected to not only a third term but to a fourth term as well.

"Trotsky's analysis was incorrect as any Monday morning quarterback can plainly see."

Hold on there, Monday morning quarterbacks. That's an illegal play and you've got to bring the ball back and take a penalty. When Trotsky made that prediction about Roosevelt, what was he doing, trying to read tea leaves? Or cast a horoscope for Roosevelt? Isn't it proper for us as disciples of Trotsky to ask ourselves what theoretical considerations led to these conclusions?

Roosevelt came into power as the representative primarily of light industry, that section of the capitalist class interested first of all in the New Deal. By 1938, when the discussion in question was held, the New Deal had pretty well run its course. This was indicated by the economic downturn of 1937 and by the development of a fascist movement in America as a reflex to the formation of the CIO and its objective tendency toward independent political action. But it is a general law of politics, as I indicated at the beginning of this article, that the personal fate of politicians is bound up with the grouping and even current in a grouping they represent. To say that "A third term for Roosevelt is absolutely excluded" is simply to personalize an abstract theoretical conclusion—the New Deal is finished.

Was Trotsky right in drawing that conclusion? In 1938 it was quite clear that a fascist movement was on the rise and it was therefore legitimate to also conclude that "It is absolutely certain that Roosevelt will observe that now in the crisis he can do nothing with democratic means."

What happened? A little item that Vern and Ryan leave out—the outbreak of the Second World War. This sliced right through all the trends and along with it the Marxist projections of those trends. Roosevelt won his third and fourth terms on *that basis.* But he confirmed Trotsky nevertheless by announcing himself that the New Deal was dead. And as for continuing to rule by the "accustomed bourgeois democratic methods," as Vern and Ryan declare, Roosevelt violated them in principle not only by breaking his campaign promise to keep out of war but by turning to decree rule, slapping on a wage freeze, persecuting the miners union; and, we may add, by imprisoning the Trotskyists for exercising their democratic right to oppose imperialist war and advocate socialism. The Bonapartist element in the Roosevelt regime grew considerably. As for the fascist movement, it was cut off short, not to resume until the world conflict came to an end.

Studying Trotsky's error, then, we see that it was one of form and not of substance. Trotsky was aware, we may be sure, that a certain amount of political risk was involved in choosing the form he did for making his prediction. On the other hand the chances for political gain were considerable. And since only something as major as a world war could affect it, that kind of error could be handled without too great disadvantage. It took the new world war Trotsky had predicted to cancel out his prediction Roosevelt would not serve a third term!

But let us continue with the correction offered by our Monday morning quarterbacks. They see Trotsky's error as "two-fold." First it was an error *"in tempo."* Trotsky's forecast about "the inability of the American bourgeoisie to rule indefinitely with democratic means" came true much later than he expected. The worth of that "correction" can be judged in the light of the failure of Vern and Ryan to consider the intervention of World War II. They just don't know what they are talking about.

Secondly, "Trotsky's error in the tempo of events may very well have derived from his other error which consists in *a misconception as to what Hague was and represented in New Jersey."* We are then informed that "Trotsky's error in tempo derived from misinformation as to the nature of Hague's political activity and the forces upon which it was based." Where Vern and Ryan got this information remains a top-drawer secret. I had the rare good fortune and privilege to work with Trotsky and I can assure his correctors that he was very well informed. He not only read the *New York Times* the same as Ryan (if I recall the discussion correctly, Trotsky's reference, "I read about the tactics of Hague," was to the *New York Times*) but he was in correspondence with Marxists in the U.S. well able to separate fact from fiction, read the American Trotskyist press closely, and was also visited by any number of Americans, both Marxist and otherwise, who reported what was happening.

The truth is that our Monday morning quarterbacks feel quite correctly that their method, based on their information, would never reveal Hague as a fascist. First of all, Hague, according to them, did not have his own gang. Secondly, Hague did not represent the small bosses, for this "would inevitably have been expressed in the formulation of some sort of 'radical' or 'anti-capitalist' program. . . ." And so—Trotsky must have been wrong. Hague wasn't a fascist. He must have been just a "bourgeois democrat."

Permit me to set the facts straight by quoting from a letter from a participant in the struggle against Hague, George Breitman:

"I leave aside the question of whether Hague represented 'small bosses who became infuriated because the crisis deepened.' (The key here is the meaning of the word 'represented.' I am inclined to think that Trotsky's estimate on this was fundamentally sound.) All I deal with here is the question of extra-legal gangs.

"Hague, it is true, had an understanding with the racketeer-ridden AFL and therefore felt no need to try to destroy the AFL unions immediately, but that doesn't mean he wasn't out to destroy the union movement as a whole ultimately. His main target was the CIO for the time being since it was the CIO that represented the real threat then. Vern-Ryan say, 'In this endeavor Hague did not employ "his own gang" which is absolutely unconstitutional but the Jersey City Police and Democratic Party hangers-on, sworn in as special police and deputies. This use of the police was as unconstitutional as is their usual use in labor disputes; but there is a qualitative difference between using a legal armed body in an unconstitutional fashion and forming an unconstitutional armed body as the nucleus of a "new" state.'

"What are the facts? Hague did use the police in unconstitutional activities. On occasion he also swore in deputies, etc. But he did more than that. He also organized his own gangs, and these gangs were used to cow and beat up or drive out of town organizers, leaflet distributors, speakers, etc. In 1939 (June 4) one of these gangs even traveled to Newark to break up an open-air meeting Norman Thomas was to address. (See pamphlet, *The Fight Against Hagueism*.) These weren't deputies or cops, but a gang. Previously the CIO and other groups trying to organize Jersey City decided to organize a free-speech meeting. (See pp. 3–4 of same pamphlet.) Hague had not only his cops and deputies there but thousands of people whipped up by his gang—including all the veterans, carrying clubs. The result was that two members of the U.S. Congress did not dare to even enter Jersey City to speak there. Another attempt was made. (See pp. 4–5.) Our party participated actively in this one. Through us an incipient workers defense guard movement was started, with the Newark CIO and Workers Alliance agreeing to provide support for the congressman who was to defy Hague. I was there in Pershing Field with one of the Workers Alliance guards. But the whole thing fell through due to political timidity and poor organization. Thousands of people roamed the field, most of them in well organized bands, led by Legionnaires carrying clubs. The minute O'Connell was spotted he was grabbed and slammed into a car, banging his arm brutally on the way, and he was run out of town. An assistant CIO regional director was treated even worse, being beaten so badly he had to be hospitalized. It wasn't the cops or deputies that did this.

"Such are the things Trotsky was talking about, and he was absolutely right when he called them unconstitutional gangs. The trouble with Vern and Ryan is that they don't know what they are talking about on this matter, or if they did know, have forgotten facts that were well known at the time Trotsky made his estimate of Hague as a fascist. These bands were not made permanent because the war came, the Stalinists became pro-war and even pro-Hague, openly supporting his candidates, and Hague, in return for their tolerance and Roosevelt's, decided that he could get along with the CIO. In other words, Hague changed. But before he changed, he definitely followed the fascist pattern in his organization of extra-legal bands to war on the CIO."

Now that the facts are clear, perhaps Vern and Ryan will feel half willing to change their estimate of Hague. Half willing, because the "bourgeois democrat" Hague definitely had one of the "two inescapable and basically essential features" of a fascist, he had "his own gang." It is tempting to leave it to Vern and Ryan to puzzle out whether Trotsky committed a half error or whether Hague didn't somehow or other have the second "inescapable and basically essential" feature they need to tell a fascist from a liberal, but perhaps we should suggest a way out of their dilemma. Doesn't Hague's whole course of action itself constitute a program with eloquent appeal to the "small bosses who became infuriated because the crisis deepened"?

Now let me demonstrate how completely beside the point this whole elaborate attempt to pontificate on Trotsky's "error" really is. "In a fit of impatience to be about the settlement of tasks not yet posed by history," Vern and Ryan declare, "well intentioned comrades run the risk of ignoring or misapplying the science of Marxism. In picking up the error that Trotsky committed in regard to Hague, they unconsciously turn a great revolutionist into a prop for the bourgeois order: if Hague was a fascist, then

McCarthy is also; the class struggle is developed, then, not so much against the bourgeois state as against this 'fascism' of one of its parliamentary bodies." Note that phrase, "if Hague was a fascist, then McCarthy is also...." But that was not at all the analogy drawn in the draft resolution. Our analysis of McCarthyism does not rest on such an analogy but on observation of the McCarthyite movement itself and general theoretical considerations. The analogy with Hague concerns the possibility of McCarthy *ceasing to be a fascist.* "It is not excluded," we said, "that McCarthy and those around him can be absorbed by the Republican machine.... This type of withdrawal was seen in the case of Mayor Hague, a potential candidate for the role of American Hitler in the late thirties. But if McCarthy follows this course, the role of fascist leader will fall to someone else who will pick up the strings by denouncing McCarthy's 'treason and betrayal.'"

Isn't it clear that Vern and Ryan were so busy nailing together a jerry-rigged platform of opposition that they couldn't even read straight? They didn't even notice that magic word, "potential," qualifying the candidacy of Mayor Hague, not to speak of the fact that as an example, and there are such, of a "bourgeois democrat" changing into a fascist, Hague meets their criteria rather well, or should we say half well?

By the way, while we are on the point it would undoubtedly prove instructive to hear from Vern and Ryan on how their "two inescapable and basically essential features" for telling a fascist apply to General Franco. The Spanish Generalissimo had the armed gangs without doubt, but how about a "radical" or "anti-capitalist" program? Having "corrected" Trotsky on Hague, it seems in order for them to proceed a bit further and "correct" him also on Franco. Perhaps Trotsky's "error"—or half-error—in regard to Franco also "derived from misinformation" as in the case of Hague?

## Why we call McCarthyism 'incipient' fascism

In contrast to this tangle of errors, confusion and misinformation, let me summarize the approach used in the draft resolution. McCarthy's whole course of action reveals his aim—the destruction of bourgeois democratic forms. Once this aim was clearly revealed, it was sufficient to demarcate him from the bourgeois democrats. And as soon as it became clear that his principal means to achieve this was the organization of a middle-class following independently of the Republican and Democratic machines, we had sufficient criteria to characterize him as a fascist. But if we are prepared to call McCarthyism "fascism," why do we put the adjective "incipient" in front of it?

The reason is that although McCarthyism is fascism in essence it is far from being fully formed. It has not even built its own party. At present it exists as a faction primarily in the Republican Party but also extending into Democratic ranks. This stage of its existence still remains to be completed. Therefore, in form it is not yet an independent organization. Its propaganda likewise is far from finished form. And the same goes for its extra-legal squads and activities.

If Vern and Ryan can follow the analogy, it is incipient fascism the way a crocodile egg is an incipient crocodile. Although the egg has a form that enables us to recognize what species and genus it belongs to, thereby enabling us to differentiate it from say an egg laid by a liberal goose, it lacks completely the shape and articulation of the adult animal. Naturally, to people accustomed to approaching such phenomena solely with a frying pan or griddle in mind, the distinction is of little value. For them the important thing is to be able to recognize an egg when you see it. In the case of McCarthy, however, I would say the egg has about hatched, giving us sight of a reptile that shows little inclination to passively accept being whipped up into a liberal omelette.

Having determined what McCarthyism is in essence, it is not too difficult to determine the tendencies of its evolution, for these will all be toward the development of fascism in its full-fledged form, with such modifications as the American scene imposes. Thus McCarthy's factional activities indicate the trend toward independent organization. His "treason" and "communist menace" themes indicate the trend toward social demagogy, as does his use of the big lie technique. (Note to Vern and Ryan: The political need to appear anti-capitalist is not so pressing for McCarthy as it was for Hitler, who faced a Social Democratic and Communist movement having millions of members and influencing tens of millions more.) The links already formed between him and the conscious fascist groupings about the country, the racists, Legionnaires, and so on, project in no direction except the formation of gangs such as formed around Hague and Coughlin. (Here, I must observe that it would be the most criminal irresponsibility to assure the Jews, Negroes and foreign born, as do Vern and Ryan, that American fascism does not have "a pre-determined attitude" toward them—that it might not even be officially "anti-USSR or anti-Stalinist"! To make such assurances would be nothing less than to assist in disarming the first prospective victims of McCarthyism.)

How impelling these tendencies become will depend finally of course upon far greater forces than the McCarthyite movement in and of itself. The political resolution considers these in the order of their importance. First of all, is America's world position. If you grant that America's relative world position has been seriously weakened by the development of revolutionary movements abroad, then with iron logic it follows that this weakening will have a domestic reflex in greatly heightened economic, social, and political tensions. But after the experience of two world wars and the depression of the thirties, this can only signify a mortal crisis for American capitalism.

The socialist solution is put on the order of the day. But both theory and experience teaches that the American capitalist class can be expected to put up the most desperate resistance, and even choose a suicidal course analogous to that taken by the German bourgeoisie. The growth of McCarthyism, expressing the anguish and despair of the middle class, would begin to press actively on Big Business, seeking a decision from the ruling class to turn to action. Under such conditions it would be foolhardy to say in advance that Big Business would not yield to the pressure and go down to their doom eyes shut, but dragging a great deal along with them.

Fortunately for America and the world, Big Business and McCarthyism will not come to that unchallenged. American labor will be granted its historic opportunity and will surely justify the judgment of every great Marxist that it is the most dynamic in the world. And the American Trotskyists will do their part to assure success by offering a program of action based on a truly scientific analysis of the reality we face. That happens to include a correct analysis of McCarthyism as the American form of fascism.

# CAPITALIST CRISIS AND THE FIGHT FOR WORKERS POWER

### Imperialism's March toward Fascism and War
JACK BARNES

"There will be new Hitlers, new Mussolinis. That is inevitable. What is not inevitable is that they will triumph. The working-class vanguard will organize our class to fight back against the devastating toll we are made to pay for the capitalist crisis. The future of humanity will be decided in the contest between these contending class forces." In *New International* no. 10. $14. Also in Spanish, French, Farsi, Greek.

### Fascism: What It Is and How to Fight It
LEON TROTSKY

Writing in the heat of struggle against the rising fascist movement in Europe in the 1930s, Russian communist leader Leon Trotsky examines the origins and nature of fascism and advances, for the first time, a working-class strategy to combat and defeat it. $5. Also in French and Farsi.

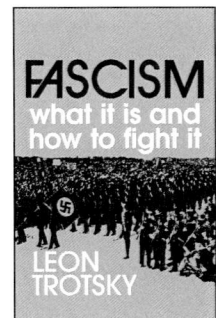

### Fascism and Big Business
DANIEL GUERIN

Examines the development of fascism in Germany and Italy and its relationship with the ruling capitalist families there. $20

### Are They Rich Because They're Smart?
**Class, Privilege, and Learning under Capitalism**
JACK BARNES

Exposes growing class inequalities in the US and the self-serving rationalizations of well-paid professionals who think their "brilliance" equips them to "regulate" working people, who don't know what's in our own best interest. $10. Also in Spanish, French, Farsi, Arabic.

### Is Socialist Revolution in the US Possible?
**A Necessary Debate among Working People**
MARY-ALICE WATERS

Fighting for a society only working people can create, it is our own capacities we will discover. And we will answer the question posed here with a resounding "Yes." Revolution is possible but not inevitable. That depends on us. $7. Also in Spanish, French, Farsi.

### The Clintons' Anti-Working-Class Record
**Why Washington Fears Working People**
JACK BARNES

What working people need to know about the profit-driven course of Democrats and Republicans alike over the last three decades. And the political awakening of workers seeking to understand and resist the capitalist rulers' assaults. $10. Also in Spanish, French, Farsi, Greek.

### Cuba and the Coming American Revolution
JACK BARNES

This is a book about the example set by the Cuban people that revolution is not only necessary—it can be made. A book about the struggles of workers and other exploited producers in the imperialist heartland, and the youth attracted to them. About the class struggle in the US, where the revolutionary capacities of working people are as utterly discounted by the ruling powers as were those of the Cuban toilers. And just as wrongly. $10. Also in Spanish, French, Farsi.

PATHFINDERPRESS.COM

# Also from Pathfinder

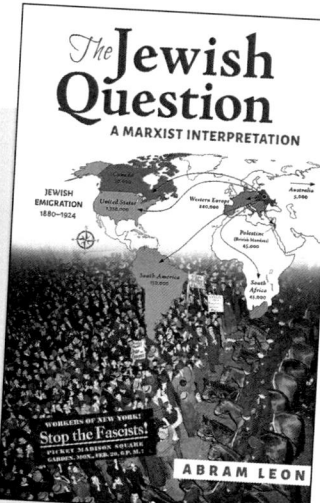

## The Jewish Question
A MARXIST INTERPRETATION
*Abram Leon*

The battle against reactionary forces aiming to exterminate the Jews remains central to world politics, as shown by the genocidal October 2023 pogrom in Israel. Why is Jew-hatred still raising its ugly head? What are its class roots? Why, as Abram Leon explains, is there no solution "independent of the world proletarian revolution"? Revised translation, new introduction, and 40 pages of illustrations and maps. $17. Also in Spanish and French.

## The Communist Manifesto
*Karl Marx and Frederick Engels*

Communism, say the founding leaders of the revolutionary workers movement, is not a set of ideas or preconceived "principles" but workers' line of march to power, springing from a "movement going on under our very eyes." $5. Also in Spanish, French, Farsi, Arabic.

## The Teamster Series
*Farrell Dobbs*

Four books on the strikes, organizing drives, and political campaigns that transformed the Teamsters across the Midwest in the 1930s into a militant industrial union movement. Written by Farrell Dobbs, the general organizer of these Teamster battles and leader of the Socialist Workers Party.

A tool for workers seeking to use union power in every workplace and advance the fight for an independent labor party. $16 each, series $50. Also in Spanish. *Teamster Rebellion* is also available in French, Farsi, Greek.

## Malcolm X Talks to Young People

"The young generation of whites, Blacks, browns, whatever else—you're living at a time of revolution," said Malcolm in 1964. "And I for one will join with anyone, I don't care what color you are, as long as you want to change this miserable condition that exists on this earth." Four talks and an interview in the last months of Malcolm's life. $12. Also in Spanish, French, Farsi, Greek.

# New International
### A MAGAZINE OF MARXIST POLITICS AND THEORY

### OPENING GUNS OF WORLD WAR III: WASHINGTON'S ASSAULT ON IRAQ
JACK BARNES

The murderous assault on Iraq in 1990–91 heralded increasingly sharp conflicts among imperialist powers, growing instability of capitalism, and more wars. Also includes:
**1945: When US Troops Said No!**
by Mary-Alice Waters
**Lessons from the Iran-Iraq War**
by Samad Sharif
In *New International* no. 7. $14. Also in Spanish, French, Farsi.

### CAPITALISM'S LONG HOT WINTER HAS BEGUN
JACK BARNES

Today's global capitalist crisis is but the opening stage of decades of economic, financial, and social convulsions and class battles. Class-conscious workers confront this historic turning point for imperialism with confidence, Jack Barnes writes, drawing satisfaction from being "in their face" as we chart a revolutionary course to take power. In *New International* no. 12. $14. Also in Spanish, French, Farsi, Arabic, Greek.

### U.S. IMPERIALISM HAS LOST THE COLD WAR
JACK BARNES

The collapse of regimes across Eastern Europe and the USSR claiming to be communist did not mean workers and farmers there had been crushed. In today's sharpening class conflicts and wars, these toilers are joining working people the world over in the class struggle against capitalist exploitation. In *New International* no. 11. $14. Also in Spanish, French, Farsi, Greek.

## The Low Point of Labor Resistance Is Behind Us
THE SOCIALIST WORKERS PARTY LOOKS FORWARD

*Jack Barnes*
*Mary-Alice Waters*
*Steve Clark*

The global order imposed by Washington after its victory in World War II is shattering. A long retreat by the working class and unions has come to an end. The bosses and their government are stepping up attacks on our wages, conditions, and constitutional rights. This book highlights opportunities for building a mass proletarian party able to lead the struggle to end capitalist rule, opening a socialist future for humanity. $10. Also in Spanish and French.

## Labor, Nature, and the Evolution of Humanity
THE LONG VIEW OF HISTORY

*Frederick Engels, Karl Marx*
*George Novack, Mary-Alice Waters*

Without understanding that social labor, transforming nature, has driven humanity's evolution for millions of years, working people are unable to see beyond the capitalist epoch of class exploitation that warps all human relations, ideas, and values. Only the revolutionary conquest of state power by the working class can open the door to a world free of capitalist exploitation, degradation of nature, subjugation of women, racism, and war. A world built on human solidarity. A socialist world. $12. Also in Spanish and French.

## America's Revolutionary Heritage
MARXIST ESSAYS

*George Novack*

A materialist explanation of the American Revolution, Civil War and Radical Reconstruction, genocide against the Indians, rise of American imperialism, first wave of the fight for women's rights, and more. $23

**PATHFINDERPRESS.COM**

# EXPAND YOUR REVOLUTIONARY LIBRARY

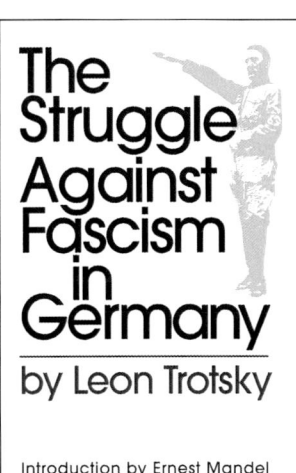

### The Struggle against Fascism in Germany
LEON TROTSKY

Writing in the heat of struggle against the rising Nazi movement, a central leader of the Bolshevik Revolution in Russia draws lessons from that first victorious proletarian revolution, examines the petty-bourgeois class roots of fascism, and presents a revolutionary political course to defeat it. $25

*New edition!*
### Che Guevara on Economics and Politics in the Transition to Socialism
CARLOS TABLADA

It's essential for working people to win state power, said Ernesto Che Guevara. "Then there's the second stage, maybe more difficult than the first"—the transition from dog-eat-dog capitalism to socialism. That includes moving from work as a condition for survival, to voluntary social labor through which we express our common humanity. Includes Fidel Castro's 1987 speech "Che's Ideas are Absolutely Relevant Today." New edition with substantially expanded selections from Guevara's writings. $17. Also in Spanish, coming in French.

### Counter-Mobilization
**A Strategy to Fight Racist and Fascist Attacks**
FARRELL DOBBS

A discussion on strategy and tactics in the fight against fascist attacks on the labor movement, drawing on the experiences of the Minneapolis Teamsters movement of the 1930s. $5

### Women in Cuba: The Making of a Revolution within the Revolution
VILMA ESPÍN, ASELA DE LOS SANTOS YOLANDA FERRER

The integration of women in the ranks and leadership of the Cuban Revolution was intertwined with the proletarian course of the leadership of the revolution from the start. This is the story of that revolution and how it transformed the women and men who made it. $17. Also in Spanish, Farsi, Greek.

### Socialism on Trial
**Testimony at Minneapolis Sedition Trial**
JAMES P. CANNON

The revolutionary program of the working class, presented in response to frame-up charges of "seditious conspiracy" in 1941, on the eve of US entry into World War II. The defendants were leaders of the Minneapolis labor movement and the Socialist Workers Party. $15. Also in Spanish, French, Farsi.

### Leon Trotsky on France

An assessment of the social and economic crisis that shook France in the mid-1930s in the aftermath of Hitler's rise to power in Germany, and a program to unite the working class and exploited peasantry to confront it. $17

---

**Pathfinder Press accessible ebooks** for the blind, those with low vision, or other challenges reading print books

For a list of current accessible titles, go to: pathfinderpress.com/collections/books-for-the-blind.

Visit Bookshare.org for information on how to sign up.

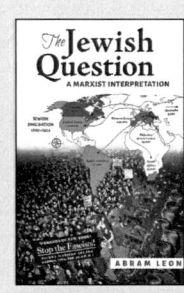